Julia A Mathews

Frank Austin's Diamond

Julia A Mathews

Frank Austin's Diamond

ISBN/EAN: 9783743319462

Manufactured in Europe, USA, Canada, Australia, Japa

Cover: Foto ©ninafisch / pixelio.de

Manufactured and distributed by brebook publishing software (www.brebook.com)

Julia A Mathews

Frank Austin's Diamond

CONTENTS.

		PAGE
I.	The Picnic	7
II.	Mountain Lake	28
III.	The Diamond in the Rough	49
IV.	Milward's Corner	73
V.	Mary Allen	97
VI.	In the Old Barn	117
VII.	Joe Milward's Visit	142
VIII.	A Flash of the Diamond	157
IX.	Hidden Manna	175

FRANK AUSTIN'S DIAMOND.

I.

THE PICNIC.

"HOLLOA, there, you lazy fellows! Get up! It's morning!"

"Oh, do stop, Will Seaton!" droned a sleepy voice from a corner of the long dormitory, through which the shrill call had resounded.

But the first speaker was not to be so easily silenced. In another moment, the bed of his slumberous companion was stripped of coverlet, sheet, and pillows, and the occupant thereof dragged from it with a sudden jerk which put his dreams effectually to flight.

"Seaton, Seaton! Come to order at once, sir," said the voice of Mr. Upton, the usher, who had been wakened from his morning nap by the uproar. "You are forgetting all discipline!"

"Oh, hear Uppy trying to come the Bentley dodge!" cried the irrepressible Will. "It won't do, Uppy; you are laughing this minute, — you know you are. You can't talk discipline in Professor Bentley's style, to save yourself. You love me too well to frown upon me, jolliest of ushers!" and with a rush and a spring, he was on Mr. Upton's bed in a twinkling. "Look out of that window and see how the clouds are breaking, and then lie abed if you can. Didn't I tell you that we'd have a bright day? Come on, all who want to go to Mountain Lake."

"Stop, Seaton!" said Mr. Upton, as the boy would have sprung off the bed again. "Those clouds are simply shifting a little; they are not passing away. Why, my boy, this is no fit day to set out on such an expedition. We must wait until to-morrow. I am sorry for you all," for the blank faces about him betokened no little disappointment, " but Dr. Drayton will give us holiday to-morrow instead."

But "to-morrow" is nothing to an eager school-boy who has been promised a holiday to-day; and these boys had been promised not only a holiday, but a grand expedition through the woods and over the rocks, ending in a picnic on a lake which lay half-way up the highest mountain in all the country round.

The very idea of to-morrow was laughed at, hooted at, or grumbled at, by each and every boy in the dormitory, all of whom, now fully roused, were hurriedly dressing; for the expedition had been ordered to start at five o'clock. The dark morning had deceived them somewhat as to the hour of rising; and woe be to the Drayton boy who was behind time in a frolic, no less than in the study-hall or class-room. The doctor's watch was never slow, and the doctor never waited an instant for a tardy boy, after its inexorable hand touched the hour.

As the occupants of the "long dormitory," — as the room in which Will Seaton and his comrades slept was called, — reached the outer hall, they were joined by crowds of their school-fellows from the other apartments, all earnestly discussing, like themselves, the weather and the prospects for the picnic.

The clouds hung heavily overhead, broken here and there by little rifts just large enough to excuse the hopes of the most sanguine, but too small and too soon hidden again to cheer the more despondent. All about the roads around the Hall stood the great farm-wagons which had been hired for the occasion, the wagoners eying the heavens askance, somewhat discontented with the thought that, having had to keep their teams in the village over night, in order to be in readiness for the early start, they seemed likely to be disappointed of their work. Among them and around them stood the boys,— some hopeful, some despairing, some sulky, some full of jokes and pranks, — all eagerly watching for the stroke of five; for that would bring Dr. Drayton, and Dr. Drayton would say yes or no, and the matter would be decided.

"Oh, he'll say go. Of course he will," said Will Seaton. "He never backs down."

"But he's wondrous prudent, Will," said Ned Churchill, who stood near him.

"And wondrous weather-wise," said Laurence Bronson. "If the doctor says that it will storm, I shall think we had better wait, much as I want to go."

"Oh, he'll be sure it's going to storm, I know that well enough," said a surly voice behind the group; and turning, the boys saw Albert Semmons.

"It will rain, of course," he went on in the same tone. "It always does when we want to do any thing."

"'All de world am sad and weary,'" chanted

Will, in such exact imitation of Albert's doleful voice, that the boys broke into a shout of laughter so loud and merry that they did not hear the sharp stroke of five from the old clock in the hall, nor see the tall figure which at that very moment took its stand on the piazza.

The first intimation they had of Dr. Drayton's presence was the sound of a loud voice, saying, " The wagons may be made ready at once. Young gentlemen, you will do well to take something to eat before we start on our long drive."

A low murmur, breaking after an instant into loud cheers for the doctor, told whether the decision was a welcome one or not, and the boys flocked into the dining-room in a body.

Ten minutes after, they were all crowding into the wagons, a noisy, tumultuous multitude, their wildest shouts and most mischievous tricks all unrebuked and unrestrained; for the doctor had made up his mind that the long talked of expedition should be a thorough and genuine frolic, and had given orders that all liberty consistent with safety to life and limb should be given to the merry-makers.

"Holloa, Churchill! There's Miss Mary," cried Laurence Bronson, as a carriage was driven into the grounds. "Now, it's sure to clear."

A little lady, with a sunny face, leaned out of the carriage as Ned sprang down the hill to meet it.

"All ready for your ride, eh?" she said. "Does Dr. Drayton think we shall have a fine day?"

"I don't know," said Ned, catching her in his arms and lifting her down as if she had been a child, holding her just long enough to give her a quick kiss on either cheek. "He says go, — so go it is. You won't care if you do get a little wetting, will you, Mary?"

"No, indeed, not I. Where is Mrs. Drayton?"

"In the library, waiting for you. She asked me just now if I thought you would be here, and I told her I was sure you would come. There she is, coming down with the doctor."

There were only three ladies in the party, — Mrs. Drayton, Mrs. Leonard, the wife of the minister, and Miss Mary Churchill; but as these were all great favorites with the boys, they were considered quite sufficient.

The packing of baskets, boxes, and bags, — not to speak of boys, — was at length completed; and the long train of wagons started off, led by the largest of them all, an immense affair, drawn by four horses, and painted bright red, looking, as Mary Churchill said, very much like the advance guard of a circus caravan. This magnificent vehicle had been claimed by each and every clique of boys in the school; but, having at length been seized by force of arms by a detachment of the senior class, had been yielded to the use of the ladies, Mr. Leonard, and Dr. Drayton,— the remainder of the seats being occupied by members of the class. Ned Churchill, Frank Austin, Laurence Bronson, Will Seaton, and a score more, sat packed like sardines in a case; but all were too jolly and happy to complain of any discomfort, and the flow of laughter, jokes, and fun, ran on, spite of the drizzling rain which had begun to fall just as they left Drayton Hall.

"I do believe we are riding right into the rain," said Frank Austin, with a mischievous chuckle of delight. "Look over on the mountains. Don't you see how it is pouring down there? I guess old Prof. will find he has made a mistake this time. Never mind, we'll have a ride, any way."

"And if we have to give it up, we'll invite him up to the barn to eat cold wittles," put in Will Seaton. "Oh, just look there!"

The heavy rain, that had been falling on the mountains which raised their tall heads before them, had suddenly ceased. The clouds had broken, and were beginning slowly to roll back, — gray billow piled upon gray billow in heavy swells, untouched as yet by any clearer light, but surging and rolling, wave upon wave, like a mighty ocean. The curious spectacle had drawn all eyes to the mountains, and the wildest of the gay party were awed and hushed by the grand sight. All at once the billowy masses of cloud were touched and tinted here and there by a rosy glow, which widened and spread until the whole dark mass was transformed into a sunny sea, which surged over the mountain-tops and broke, disclosing bits of bright blue sky beyond; then closed again, again to part as if in joyous frolic. Suddenly, with one mad, last leap, the glowing waves rushed apart, rolled heavily down the fair blue walls on either side, and lay at their base, the pink light fading slowly out, leaving them like snow-drifts on the far horizon.

A great stillness had fallen on the whole party. For a moment even Will Seaton felt the influence of the beautiful scene which they had witnessed; but only for a moment. Determined to break the spell, he sprang quickly to his feet, shouting out at the top of his strong voice, —

> "All de world am bright and sunny,
> Ebery road we take;
> Oh, fellows, we must all be funny,
> Going up to Mountain Lake."

A shout of laughter followed the impromptu lines, and Will's ruse proved a decided success; for the happy hearts all overflowed again, and the fun "ran fast and furious," only heightened by the brilliant sunshine that now bathed mountains, streams, and valleys, in its glorious light.

"Wouldn't it be jolly fun to take old Christy up with us?" said Will. "There he is now with the two boys. Let's ask the doctor."

"Dr. Drayton, may we take Christy and the boys up to the lake?" he asked, as the old fisherman and the two lads who stood with him on the beach waved their hats to the happy party.

"I have no objection, if they can come away at once," said Dr. Drayton.

That point was quickly settled, and the three were soon seated in the second wagon, greatly to the delight of the whole company; for Christy and his boys were prime favorites with the entire school.

A ride of fourteen miles brought them to the foot of the mountain; when every boy in the various wagons sprang out to relieve the horses, and to rest his own cramped limbs by a scramble up the rough road. What with berries to pick, rabbits to be chased, squirrels to be hunted, and so forth, the ascent was a slow affair in one sense; but, although the toiling horses often left the pleasure-seekers far behind, a fleet race soon brought the laggards up with the more sober part of the company, to be again left behind, as some new object of interest caught their attention.

"And who is this who makes his way by himself alone?" asked Mr. Grau, the German professor; who, busy in collecting specimens for a beautiful herbarium in which his soul delighted, had walked on for full four miles up the zigzag road, quite undisturbed by the shouts and capers of his light-hearted companions. "Ah, Mr. Bentley," he added, as the boy whom he addressed slightly turned his head. "It is much your custom, I perceive, to make solitary yourself. Why for do you not run to squirrels and berries as your young friends?"

"I don't care for that sort of thing," replied Bentley, without pausing in his walk.

"But it is not well for you so much to live alone," said the teacher, walking on by his side. "Look at Seaton,—merry-heart,— how he springs and laughs! He is too much life, but you are too leetle. He give you leetle of his joke, that be healthy for you; you give him leetle of your sober, that be very healthy for him. You say so?"

An expression of such intense pain crossed the face into which he looked, that Mr. Grau laid his hand upon the boy, saying gently, "I pain you? Forgive me. I say no more;" and trotted off on his short little legs, remorseful and self-reproachful, to collect more specimens.

He had been but a short time in the school, or he would have known that Will Seaton, once Arthur Bentley's sworn friend and defender, was now his unrelenting foe; and that Arthur, having lost this, his only friend, by an act of wickedness and meanness which high-minded Will could never forgive, was left desolate and solitary in that great school of three hundred boys. Poor fellow! He had committed a wicked, cruel deed, and his punishment was terrible. It was not only that he was forced to spend his life in a community of boys who hated and despised him for what he had done; but his lonely heart, which had clung so closely to this one idol, had been flung contemptuously aside as a mean, worthless thing, unfit to be loved or trusted. He deserved it, perhaps; but if we all had our deserts proportioned to our opportunities, there are many beside poor Arthur Bentley who would go through the world with aching hearts, and, perhaps, wrecked lives.

"Now, young fellows, jump in!" shouted the voice of Farmer Sanford, the driver of the first wagon and the captain of the expedition. "The worst is over now, and if you go on much longer at this rate you'll wear the legs off you before we get to the lake. That would be a pity too, for you'll need 'em bad enough when we get there."

As Mr. Grau took his seat in answer to the order which all were ready to obey, his eye happened to rest on Arthur Bentley, who was slowly approaching the wagon in which he sat. Arthur had already passed some three or four wagons, but no one had moved to make room for him, or seemed to notice his presence in any way. With a face whose dark expression seemed to gather gloom with every step, the boy went on until Mr. Grau's voice arrested him.

"Friend Bentley, will you sit side of me? I have to show you some rare plants I find in dese woods."

The brisk little man moved to make room for him with such suddenness and vigor that Tom Morrison, one of Bentley's classmates, who sat beside him, was almost pushed from his seat.

"Oh, pardon, pardon! a tousand times pardon. I have you too much crowd. So. Now we shall be — what is dat word? — fix? Yes, now we shall be very well fix;" and having moved nearer to Bentley, the friendly Grau turned first to one and then to the other of his companions, beaming upon them with a face of the utmost delight and enjoyment.

But Bentley, who had visibly brightened at the kindness shown him, looked as moody as ever as his eyes rested on Tom Morrison, and Tom seemed scarcely better pleased. Mr. Grau began to doubt the expediency of his manœuvre for drawing Arthur into closer companionship with his school-mates; but he persevered in his attempt nevertheless.

Taking out some of the beautiful specimens which he had gathered for his herbarium, he began to exhibit and describe them in a manner which won the interest of both boys; and ere long, to his great satisfaction, he had succeeded in provoking a discussion between them in which they seemed to forget the differences which had separated them. Both were good botanists, and both loved the study enthusiastically; and they grew so warm in their debate, that more than one on the seats near them caught the tones of their earnest dispute and began to join in it, taking one side or other of the question, irrespective of the fact that the hated Bentley was the head of the opposition against Morrison; while the good hearted German sat by, throwing in a word here and there to quicken the heat of the argument, smiling complacently at the success of his scheme.

Not until they came within sight of the lake, and the wild exclamations of delight from those in the forward wagons distracted their attention, did the eager talkers begin to recognize the fact that they had been holding close companionship with the boy who for months past had been ignored and set completely aside by the entire school.

But soon this ceased to be thought of, as the slow but apparently tireless horses brought them nearer and nearer to the lake;

plodding on over its stony road, with its huge wall of rock towering upon their right, and on the left shelving suddenly down in a sharp precipice which fell a hundred feet to a rocky gorge below. Before them lay the silver lake, in a basin formed on two sides by walls of rock; on the other by a high green bank which rose perpendicularly from the water, without the least slope or declivity, some thirty or forty feet; while on the side which lay toward them as they toiled up the road, the water ran gently up to the land, the tiny waves lapping softly against the grasses and overhanging branches which drooped to meet them. Clear as crystal, so transparent that every pebble-stone and every little fish swimming in its waters could be distinctly seen as you looked down into its beautiful depths, so calm and unruffled, it seemed more like some fairy lake than any thing real or commonplace.

"Let's go rowing, right away," cried Will Seaton, springing from his seat. "Come on, fellows!" and he ran toward the water, eagerly followed by a dozen of his companions.

"Stop, Seaton!" called Dr. Drayton from the first wagon. "We will have no boating until after dinner. You may all wander about here, within sound of the horn, until we have dined; then you shall go out on the lake, or anywhere else you may please. But dinner first, by all means."

The order was not an unwelcome one, much as the boys would have enjoyed an immediate trial of skill at the oars. The next half-hour was spent in loitering about in the vicinity of the lake; and when the horn called in the stragglers from their various wanderings, they gave full proof that the Doctor was not the only person in the assemblage who wanted his dinner.

Beef, chickens, bread, cake, crackers, sardines, eggs, pies, tea, coffee, biscuits, potatoes, cheese, sandwiches, ham, tongue, apples, pears, nuts, preserves, — all melted away in the most delightful manner before this array of hungry boys; until Mary Churchill — merry, sunny, little Miss Mary — fairly wore herself out with laughing over the filling and refilling of the rapidly emptied dishes and baskets.

MOUNTAIN LAKE.

"LAURENCE," said Frank Austin, linking his arm in that of Laurence Bronson, as various groups of boys began to scatter in all directions in search of different objects of interest, "what do you say to a climb up to Dragon's Head?"

"All right," said Bronson. "I'm ready. I want to go out on the lake for a row; but some of us must wait, and we may as well be among the last to take our turn."

"Anybody ready for a scramble?" shouted Frank, as they turned toward the steep and narrow footpath which led up to the Dragon's Head, — a sharp peak on the summit of the rocky cliff, which was supposed to resemble in its outlines the features of that fabulous monster.

"Ay, ay!" came back the answering call from twenty different directions, echoed and re-echoed by the reverberating rocks.

A large party, with Mr. Upton at its head, soon joined the two boys; and then began a scramble such as the hearts of boys in all ages and climes delight in. Springing over huge stones, creeping around obstructions, holding fast by a bending sapling or a shaking branch, with the delightful sense that a mis-step will end in a dangerous fall; climbing up sharp acclivities to surmount which, hand and eye, as well as practised foot, must be on the alert; creeping through rock-crevices on hands and knees; tearing their way through tangled vines and bushes, — oh! was there ever an exciting, exhilarating, adventurous walk, more dear to the soul of an enterprising boy, than the walk from Mountain Lake to Dragon's Head?

"Here we are!" cried Frank, the first to reach the summit. "Three cheers for the Dragon!"

"Three cheers for the Dragon!" shouted Edward Churchill, who was but a step behind him.

And then the whole mountain-side rang again with the clear music, as nearly fifty young voices shouted out a joyous huzza.

"Have you ever seen the lake in the cavern?" asked Mr. Upton, as he stood on the extremity of the peak with Laurence, Frank, and Ned.

Ned had seen it many a time, but Frank and Laurence had never visited the spot. Mr. Upton directed them to it, saying that, as there were only three teachers beside himself with the party, he could not accompany them. Ned offered to remain with him and help to preserve order, and the favor was gratefully accepted; for the task of keeping such a large company of adventurous boys out of danger, in such a spot, was no easy matter.

The cavern was soon found, it being but a stone's throw from the peak. Entering by a low and narrow aperture, the boys found themselves within a cave whose massive walls of stone rose all around them, forming a beautiful arch, broken at its centre as if with a blow from a huge hammer wielded by some mammoth hand. Directly below this rift lay a small sheet of water, — a tiny lake, clear and bright, rippling and shimmering in the light of a dancing sunbeam, which, falling in through the rift, struck across it from side to side. Close beside it was a rough seat, formed of stones which had fallen from the roof of the cave; and there the two boys threw themselves down to rest.

They were silent for awhile, for the quiet, solemn beauty of the spot threw its charm around them; and nearly a quarter of an hour had passed before Frank, who was the first to break the stillness, said, —

"Bronson, I mean to start a prayer-meeting down at Milward's Corner."

He spoke suddenly, with a fixed, determined sort of manner, which showed very plainly that he expected opposition, and intended to carry out his scheme in spite of it. Laurence looked at him as if he did not feel quite sure that he was in his right mind.

"At Milward's Corner!" he said at last. "Why, Austin, you'll be mobbed. There isn't such another black hole in these United States."

"All the more reason why it should be cleansed if that were so," replied Frank. "But many a place as black as the Corner has been whitened and purified by earnest men. The truth is, Bronson, I must go to work. For months past I have been calling myself a soldier of Christ, I have been enrolled in His army, I have been receiving His wages, but I have not lifted my hand to do battle for Him."

"You have been living for Him," said Laurence, gently, "and living as fair and true a Christian life, Frank, as I have ever seen."

"I have tried to follow Him," and the boy's face brightened as he spoke; "but I must do something worth while. I must have work, Larry. I lie awake at night, and plan, and think, and long, until it seems as if I never should grow quiet again. The thought struck me, one night last week, that I might do something at Milward's Corner. I jumped at it in a moment; but I don't want to be reckless, so I determined to think it over for a week before I spoke of it to any one. I have thought it over earnestly; and I have resolved to go into that den, and try to work for our Master there."

"Of course you will speak to the Doctor first?"

"Certainly I shall. I am not afraid that he will oppose it if I promise to be cautious. Hark! What is that? Are they calling us?"

"Yes, that is Ned Churchill's shout," said Laurence; as a clear, loud "Hallo, boys!" re-echoed among the cliffs again.

"All right! We're coming," he answered; and they stepped from the soft, gray twilight within the cave into the bright sunshine without.

"Down to the lake!" came back to them, in reply, from the party, who were already some distance on their way; and the two boys hurried after their comrades.

Meanwhile the lake had been the scene of an accident, which had threatened to turn the day of pleasure into one of sore distress.

The boating parties had been made up into three companies, each of which had claimed one of the ladies; and the two boats in which Mrs. Drayton and Mrs. Leonard had taken their places had received their quota of passengers, and were lying out a little from the shore, waiting for the third boat which lay at the landing.

"Now, Miss Mary, steady. The water is very deep here," said Tom Morrison, holding by one hand to the rock which, standing just a little above water-mark, formed an excellent landing spot, while he held out the other to aid Miss Churchill in stepping into the boat.

"Let me help too," cried Cuthbert Gray, — a little fellow about ten years old, who had taken a childish fancy to Mary, and had been her devoted slave all through the day, — springing to his feet, as he spoke, with a sudden jump which rocked the boat violently.

"Sit down, Cuthbert!" exclaimed Morrison, and half a dozen more; but the mischief was done.

At the very instant in which Mary stepped from the rock, the boat swayed from its moorings. Tom clung for dear life to the hand he held, and to the rock from which his fingers were fast slipping; but the loaded boat was too much for him; it swung heavily outward, and, with a little cry, Mary Churchill went down under the cold, calm water. But Tom held her fast with a grip of steel, and a white, set face, which told that all the strength of his young frame was in the grasp of the hand which held that small wrist beneath the water, as he leaned over the side of the boat, kept back by a pair of well-knit, sinewy arms which clasped his waist tightly.

There had been a loud, wild cry, — then an instant's pause, — then the leap of a lithe, active, boyish figure into the stream. Three or four bold, powerful strokes brought the swimmer to the spot, and in another moment Mary Churchill's face was lifted into the sunlight again.

"Bravo! Bravo! Hurrah for Jem Dunn!" was shouted enthusiastically, as he bore her back to the rock and lifted her into the arms outstretched to receive her.

In the midst of the shouts, Mary Churchill opened her eyes, with a little shudder and groan; but, looking up to see gentle, tender

faces bending over her, smiled back at them, and soon said, faintly enough at first, but still in her own sweet voice, that she was not hurt, only a little shaken and startled. And when Dr. Drayton threw a cloak around her, and lifting her in his arms told her she must be carried to the house at once, she looked up at him with all the old twinkle in her eyes, saying merrily, —

"You had better hang me out to dry first, sir. I feel a little damp."

But for all that, he saw, as he bent to lift her, that the bright eyes were full of tears, and he did not speak to her again; for, as he turned from the crowd and walked swiftly toward the house with his light burden, he noticed that the face grew very grave, and as the eyes looked far away to the westward, the lips moved softly, though he heard no sound; and he knew that she was thanking the watchful Master for the strong arm and the willing heart which had been ready for her in her time of need.

Down at the lake, all was for awhile eager excitement and congratulation. Tom Morrison and Jem Dunn, old Christy's grandson, were overwhelmed with praise; and even Christy himself, standing there among the crowd of excited boys, his weather-beaten face all aglow with delight at the thought that his boy had saved Miss Mary's life, received a full share of hand-shaking and congratulation.

"Who was that fellow who held on to me from behind?" asked Tom Morrison, suddenly turning from the group who had closed round him, as, having brought the boat in, he and his companions stood upon the rock from which Mary had fallen. "If it hadn't been for him I'd have been overboard, and Miss Mary would have gone to the bottom in spite of me. He's got a grip, I tell you. Why!—"

He fell back a little as his eyes met those of Arthur Bentley, who stood just beside him; for there came to him the recollection that Bentley had been behind him in the boat.

They stood and looked at one another for a moment; then Tom's better nature triumphed, and stepping quickly forward, risking, as he knew, the jeers of the whole school, he held out his hand, saying heartily, —

"Shake hands on it, old fellow. You had as much to do in saving Miss Mary as I."

"Don't say that anywhere but here," cried Bentley, grasping the proffered hand. "I did no more for her than I would have done for any living thing. Promise me to say nothing more about it, all of you," he added, turning towards the little group.

The promise was easily given, and the circumstance soon forgotten in the greater interests of the day. But it served to give Bentley another stepping-stone towards the society and companionship from which he had been for months debarred.

Never was country inn more devoid of the necessaries for fitting out a short, plump, little lady with a wardrobe than the house at Mountain Lake. The hostess was, so far as her heart was concerned, more than ready to supply Miss Mary's needs; but a short stuff-petticoat and a calico short-gown, set off by a pair of coarse leather shoes, were all that she could offer in the shape of a suit. Fortunately, Miss Mary was very easily pleased; and, replying to all the old woman's apologies by many thanks, she donned the quaint garments with all speed, hoping to be out again before Edward should reach the lake and hear of her accident.

"Look!" she said, gaily, turning to Mrs. Leonard and Mrs. Drayton, who had been assisting her in taking off her own water-soaked clothing. "I think even Ned would scarcely know me now."

"Who did you say, Miss?" asked their hostess, earnestly; but seeing that Miss Churchill had spoken to the ladies instead of to herself, as she had at first supposed, she dropped a funny little curtsy, and with a sigh went back to the task of hanging Miss Mary's garments to dry on a line she had put around the stove, in which she had built a fire when the young lady was carried up to the house.

But quickly as she had turned away her face, Miss Mary had caught its eager, questioning look; and she had heard the heavy sigh that whispered something of a grief to which the worn, furrowed face had before given her a clue.

"I was speaking of my brother, Mrs. Bailey," she said. "He is out with this party from Drayton Hall. He was up at the Dragon's Head when I fell into the lake, and I have been trying to make myself comfortable before he returned; for, although he is many years younger than I, he worries over me as if I were a child. There he is, now!"

The woman crossed the room, and stood beside her, watching the boy as he came hurrying up the road toward the house.

"Ay, but he's a likely lad," said Mrs. Bailey. "Ned,—that's the name you called him. I've a lad called Ned too, dear heart; but he's not such a one as that. But I'll not disturb you with him now," she added, as Mary looked at her with eyes in which pity for her, and gladness in her own Ned, struggled for the place. "Go out to him, dear."

She threw open the window, and Mary stepped out on a piazza. Ned was still at some distance from her, and catching sight of the little figure, in a short, blue petticoat and dark calico jacket, with a mass of curling hair falling all about its face, he ran forward, saying eagerly,—

"How is the lady? Is she at all hurt?"

"Not at all, sir," said the little girl, as he had thought her, running down the steps to meet him.

"Why,—why, Mary Churchill!" and he caught her and held her tightly, as if he were afraid she might even yet slip from him, and sink down into the quiet waters of the lake.

Mary grew grave as the close, loving grasp told her the thoughts that were in his heart.

"We must be very, very grateful, dear," she said, clinging to his arm. "I have been rescued from awful peril to-day, and we must not forget Him who saved me."

"No, indeed, the good fellow! We'll make it up to him, Mary. Jem's work this day has richly repaid all we've ever done for him or his grandfather. O Mary!" and he held her off from him and gazed at her, with a face for the moment blanched of its rosy color, "what would have become of me if they had not saved you?"

"We owe them all a world of love and gratitude, Ned; but when I spoke I was thinking of Him who gave them the power to save me;" and she looked wistfully into Ned's eyes.

But they did not brighten now as they had done before.

"Oh!" he said, almost carelessly; and then running his hand through the soft curls which fell down to her waist, he said, gaily: "Do you know you look as pretty as a picture in that queer dress, with your hair hung out to dry? 'Waving tresses, golden brown!' you'd make a lovely little peasant girl, May."

"Would I? Well, you shall paint my picture one of these days. Where are you going next? Out on the lake?"

"No, I shall stay here with you until you want to go out. Wouldn't a brisk walk warm you up?"

"I dare say it would. But I can't walk in these shoes. They are so large that I should fall on these stony paths, and add to my woes by spraining my ankle. So I will sit here in the sun with Mrs. Bailey, and you must take Mrs. Leonard and Mrs. Drayton out for a row or a walk. They are losing all their day's pleasure, shut up here with me."

Ned fell into the trap laid for him at once;

and Mary went into the house to ask the ladies, who had insisted upon staying with her, if they would not let Ned take them out.

"He will persist in remaining with me," she said, "unless he thinks he can do something for you; and then I shall feel that I have spoiled the day, not only for you, but for all those who want you to share the good time out of doors. Besides, I can see that this lonely woman here is just aching for a talk with somebody. You take Ned away, and I'll lend the poor thing an ear to pour her troubles into, in return for all her kindness to me."

So, by dint of urging and coaxing she gained her point; and in a few moments she was sitting on the steps of the piazza with Mrs. Bailey beside her, the soft September sunlight falling all around them, lighting up the storyteller's sad, furrowed brow, and shining on the lady's golden hair and sweet sympathizing face, as the old woman told, and Miss Mary listened to, the tale of a mother's love, and a son's waywardness and folly.

"Do you know where he is now?" asked Miss Churchill, as the woman ended the long, mournful story of disobedience, cruelty and final desertion.

"Yes, dear, I do indeed. You'll know Milward's Corner, perhaps? Well, it's there he is, and has been these two years. There's never as wicked a place as it is in all the country round; and he's just in the thick of it all, body and soul. And what can I do, ma'am, — me a lone widder woman?"

It was a hard question to answer, and Mary did not attempt at first to reply to it, save by stroking the withered old hand, which for the past half-hour had been lying in her lap as confidingly as if she had been the friend of a lifetime. And when she did answer it in words, they were not her own; but old, old words, spoken hundreds of years ago to other aching hearts by One who alone knew their bitterness. But old as the words were, they had all their sweetness and beauty and freshness still; and when, not long after, Ned came to tell Mary that the Doctor had ordered the wagons for the drive home, the weary, anxious mother, not only with a lightened heart, but with a quiet smile on her pale lips, left them to go into the house and fold Miss Mary's garments to be carried away.

Miss Churchill little thought as, an hour after, she sat carefully bundled up in the wagon, telling to her brother and Frank Austin — who sat on either side of her — the story she had just heard, that she was giving a young missionary a new motive for the work which he intended to perform.

And in another voice, too, there came to Frank, unconsciously to the speaker, strong, helpful words of encouragement in his undertaking. On the seat before them was Laurence Bronson, talking with old Christy; and Austin, as he listened to Miss Mary, suddenly caught the words spoken in the old fisherman's tremulous but earnest voice, —

"At Milward's Corner? God bless his brave young heart! Ah, no; don't you be afeared for him, Master Bronson. The Lord can look after his own."

But all serious thought was soon put to flight by the rollicking fun of that ride down the mountain. The shouts and laughter of the joyous party seemed to infect the horses with their own wild spirits; and spite of the heavy brakes attached to the wagons, they went down the steep, stony road at a speed which, to a stranger, would have seemed fearfully perilous. But, thoroughly trained to their work, and sure-footed as hinds, they brought their precious load in safety to the end of the apparently dangerous journey.

The moon rode high in the heavens, as, making the air ring merrily with songs and choruses, the noisy party rode into the grounds of Drayton Hall, as tired, but as happy a company as ever came home from a day's rambling.

III

THE DIAMOND IN THE ROUGH.

DR. DRAYTON was sitting in his library on the evening of the day following the excursion to Mountain Lake, his head bent low over his books, and his brow knit as if in deep study, when a quick rap upon the door changed the current of his thoughts. He lifted his head, and the whole expression of his face was altered as, in answer to his " Come," the door opened, and Frank Austin entered.

Until very lately the two had met, when circumstances brought them into close personal contact, as Dr. Drayton had always met with his pupils, — with a feeling of respectful deference on the one hand, and of care and interest on the other; but now they met as friend with friend; the lighting of the two faces, the grasp of the hands, the steady look into each other's eyes, would have told that truth to the most careless observer.

But a few months ago, Frank had gone into that study in the first flush and gladness of a new love to which his heart had heretofore been a stranger; and Dr. Drayton had received him with a sympathy and tenderness so unexpected and so full, that the boy's whole heart had gone out to him in affectionate confidence and trust. The teacher took the precious gift of that fresh young heart with a feeling of grateful joy which would have astonished even those who supposed that they knew him best; for Dr. Drayton had not the talent of winning love. Reserved, quiet, stern, and apparently cold, his boys, and almost every one with whom he had to do, looked up to him, honored him, and trusted him; but he knew — and knew it to his grief, too — that there were very few who loved him; among his scholars scarcely one.

And so it was little wonder that when this bright, glowing face showed itself at his door, and his hand was held fast in a close, loving grasp, that he should have laid his other hand upon the boy's head and stroked it fondly, as, having risen from his seat to meet him, he stood looking down into Austin's face. If those usually cold gray eyes had oftener rested on his scholars with that tender, yearning look, Dr. Drayton would not have had so great cause to mourn that he could not gain the love and confidence of the young hearts committed to his care.

"Have you a few minutes to spare to me, or will I interrupt you if I come in?" asked Frank, with an ease and freedom which showed that the Doctor's study was no new place of resort for him.

"As many minutes as you need," was the reply. "Come to the sofa, and we will talk it over; for I see that there is some subject coming up for discussion. What plan is afoot now? Another advance into the enemy's country?" and he shook his head very decidedly.

"Yes, sir; an advance into the enemy's country; but not in the way you mean. We would hardly have the coolness to ask for another holiday yet awhile. But I want to attack a real enemy, and I need your advice as to how I had best move against him. You know, Doctor," and he laid his hand on Dr. Drayton's knee, " you know that I have done nothing yet for my Captain, and I want to work for Him."

"Well, my boy, what more? You have gone farther than that."

"Yes, sir," said Austin, looking up, with a smile; "I have gone a little farther; I have determined to set up the standard at Milward's Corner, and see if I can do any thing there;" and he watched the master's face anxiously as he spoke.

He could gain nothing from it at first, for

it was simply looking back at him with an unmoved, set expression, which Frank would once have taken as a sign of utter lack of interest and appreciation. But he knew better than that now. So he sat and waited patiently for the moment when the calm, absorbed face should turn towards him, and the deep eyes should be lifted to his again. The moment came before long; and the first words that Dr. Drayton spoke proved that his apparent abstraction was only the result of the close thought he had given to Austin's new scheme.

"It might be done," he said, at length, in his slow, measured tones. "Yes, I think it might be done. But, Austin, that would be a very hard field, and you are young and quite new to the work. How do you propose to begin?"

"I have been down there reconnoitering a little," said Frank, "and I find that there is a shanty next to Milward's liquor-shop, where

I can hire a room for a few shillings a month. My idea is to hold a meeting there on Sabbath afternoons, — a sort of prayer-meeting."

" Who would assist you ? Any one among the boys ? "

" I think Bronson would help me regularly; and some of the older fellows beside would drop in once in a while, I dare say. But for constant assistance, help which could be depended on, I doubt if I would have any aid but Bronson's."

" And you two are ready to undertake it alone ? "

" I have not spoken to him yet about sharing in the plan; I simply told him that I intended to try to do something there. There is very little doubt he will help me; but if he does not see his way clear to do so, I will try it alone."

" This is a very grave work, Austin, and one which, once undertaken, must be carried out, spite of all discouragements or hardships or annoyances. You cannot let it drop after it is once started."

"I have thought of all that, sir. I do not mean to let it drop, whatever the trials connected with it may be. But it won't be all hard labor, Doctor," added the boy, his face lighting up as he spoke. "There'll be a great deal of joy and pleasure in it. There'll be such a deal of happiness in the very work itself, you know, that the trouble will be paid for as we go along."

"You must not expect too much, my son," said the doctor, smiling rather sadly at the boy's enthusiasm. "I am afraid that you will not be very well 'paid,' as you say. That corner is a terrible place. I think that you will not make much headway there. You will be disappointed if you count on a large reward."

"Oh, I meant that the task would pay for itself," said Frank, eagerly. "I don't know," he added, more quietly, "whether our Lord will let us see even one soul brought back to Him as the reward of our own personal labor; but I should think perhaps He might. Even if He does not we will still be working for *Him*. It does seem to me, doctor, that if I could only feel that I was doing some real, earnest work for Christ, I should be perfectly content. It seems as if I were just hungry for it."

"Then you will be satisfied, my son," said Dr. Drayton, gently. "There was One who said, 'My meat is to do the will of Him that sent me;' and those 'that hunger and thirst after righteousness shall be filled.' If you are hungering for a holy life, and to 'work the works' of God, you shall 'have meat to eat that others know not of.' I will not discourage you, Austin. Only be very cautious and wise. If I were in your place I would have a talk with old Christy about this thing before attempting to start it. He knows more of those people than we do, and will be better able to advise you as to the best method of commencing operations than I. Good-night, my boy."

"Good-night, sir, and thank you for all the time you have given me."

Dr. Drayton did not answer; but as Frank looked up at him, noticing his silence, he laid both his hands upon his head. The boy bent forward, and with a tremble in his voice, the master said tenderly, "The Lord bless thee and keep thee; the Lord make his face to shine upon thee and be gracious unto thee; the Lord lift up his countenance upon thee and give thee peace."

Christopher Dunn's old clock had just rung out six loud, honest strokes, as Frank Austin gave a rap on the cabin-door the next morning.

"This is an early visit, isn't it, Christy?" he asked, as the old man came to meet him, with a look of some surprise on his face. "I wanted to have a talk with you, and I did not know of any time in the day but this when we could be sure that none of the other fellows would come in upon us. So I stole out of bed without waking any one, and ran down here. Where are the boys?"

"Gone a-fishin', sir. They goes out for a bit every mornin', to get their hands in like, afore they starts off on the peddlin' with the wagon. But isn't Jem a proud fellow, Mr. Austin? He's been on the watch ever since he came to me to do a good turn for Miss Mary or Mr. Edward; not to say to pay them back for all they've done for him, but just to show his heart like. And he's that glad that he was chose as the one to save her, that he scarce knows how to explain himself. He's a strong and active swimmer, is Jem. 'Twas only a short while back that he saved another woman from drownin'."

"He is a great blessing to you, isn't he, Christy?" said Frank, as the old face glowed and sparkled with infinite delight.

"That he is, sir; that he is. And I thank the Lord for sending him to me. But what was it you came to say, Mr. Austin? I mustn't keep you yarnin' about my boy, when you've taken all this trouble to have a talk with me. What is it, sir? Nothing bad, I know by the look of you."

"No, nothing bad, Christy; but I want to ask your advice. Suppose I wanted to do something for our Master; could I find a better field to work in than Milward's Corner?"

"There's no place where there's more to do, Mr. Austin; but then again there's no place where the doin' of it would be more hard. It's a terrible bad spot, sir."

"I know it. But isn't that only another reason why I should try to make a little change in it? We mustn't pass by the dark spots, Christy, and work only in the sunshine."

"No, Mr. Frank, that we must not; and if it's your will to try what you can do for the Lord in the very midst of Satan's camp, it's not old Christy as will go agin' you. But you will need to be wise as a sarpent, sir, and harmless as a dove."

"That is just why I came to talk to you about it. I want you to tell me how to begin there. I thought of hiring a room, and holding a sociable little prayer-meeting on Sunday afternoons. Not a stiff, poky affair, you know; but a real, live, friendly meeting. Don't you think we could get it up?"

"Yes, sir; you could *get* it up; but another pint is, whether you could *keep* it up. You'd not have much help, I'm thinkin'."

"I'd keep it up if no one helped me but my Master," said the boy, stoutly.

"Then here's my hand upon it, sir; and all the aid Christy can give, you shall surely have," said the old man, heartily. "We'll do our best, Mr. Frank, and if that fails, at least our own hearts will be the warmer and the stronger for it;" and he caught Frank's hand and held it fast. "As to a place for the meetin', you might get the Widow Tracy's room, only she's very nigh hand the tavern."

"That's the very place I thought of, Christy. The fact of its being so close to the tavern is only another reason for choosing it, for some of the loungers there may stroll in once in a while."

"And you don't think they'll make you trouble, sir?"

"I should not wonder if they did try to disturb us; but our Master is stronger than theirs, and perhaps those who come in to annoy us may be won over to our side. Don't you think so?"

"I think the Lord is with you, boy, in this thing," said the old man solemnly, "and not another word will Christy say agin' it. There comes Jem now. He'll be ready with a helpin' hand for you."

Jem sat listening with a very attentive, interested face, while Frank unfolded his new plan to him; and when the earnest voice asked, in conclusion "Do you believe I can make it work, Jem?" he sat for some moments, with his chin resting on his hands, thoughtfully studying a knot-hole in a plank in the flooring, before he answered the question.

"If we only could get hold of that Ed Bailey," he said at length, "we might do something. He's the leader of that gang, and I never saw so young a chap so good at making folks do accordin' to his likin'. If we got him over, we'd have no trouble at all, for he'd make the other fellows behave themselves. But he's such a regular rowdy that I'm afraid he'll do all he can agin' us; and if he does, the rest will follow in his track."

"Ed Bailey, did you say?" asked Frank. "Is that the son of the landlady at Mountain Lake?"

"Yes, sir. He left his home entirely a year ago, because, as he said, he couldn't do as he pleased with the old woman around. He's done as he pleased since, and no mistake; for he's gone to the bad as fast as his feet could carry him. There isn't a worse fellow at the Corner (and that's sayin' a good deal) than Ed Bailey."

"Perhaps he isn't as bad as he's painted," said Frank.

"He's pretty bad, sir, accordin' to my own knowledge of him," replied Jem. "I've only been here for a few months, and of course it's only for that time I've known him; but I can see he's run a long ways down hill even in this time. He was quite a decent-lookin' young fellow when I first seen him, but now he looks worse nor any fellow of his age that I ever see. There don't seem to be a good spot in him."

"Oh, yes, there is," said Frank, cheerily. "There is a good spot in every one somewhere, and Ed Bailey must have his. Perhaps no one has tried to find it out."

"Perhaps not, Mr. Austin. Certain sure, no one ever speaks a good word for him now;

and if he did take a turn for the better, I suppose he's got none to help him. Everybody is down on him."

"Then suppose you and I take him in hand, Jem, and see if we can do any thing with him. Don't say a word yet of our intentions, but just make friends with him if you can. I will speak to him if I see him. Perhaps I can make him like me. Shall we try for it?"

"Yes, sir; for sure we will," said Jem, quickly. "I'll be proud to be workin' with you, and I'll do my part right hearty and willin.'"

"Perhaps we shall find him a diamond in the rough," and Frank laughed a musical, happy laugh.

"I don't know about the diamond, sir; but as to the rough, you'll find plenty of that. But we'll see if we can't rub him down a bit."

"All right. Now I must be off, or I shall not be at the Hall in time for prayers. I'll see you again, Christy, before I do any thing very definite. Good-by."

"Good-by, and God bless you, laddie! for if ever there was a brave young soul bent on doin' His work, 'tis yourself, Mr. Austin. Go on, boy, go on, and the dear Lord Himself go with you."

Circumstances seemed to favor Frank's plans; for, before he had walked a quarter of a mile toward the Hall, he caught sight of the figure of a man sauntering slowly up the road before him, and as he came nearer he recognized Ed Bailey. There was certainly nothing very prepossessing in the appearance of the young man. A short, thick-set figure, with broad shoulders, surmounted by a head covered with a thick crop of dark hair, which clustered in close curls over the low forehead, beneath whose heavy brows a pair of small, keen, black eyes looked sharply out upon what — to judge by the sullen, dogged expression of his face — must have been a very disagreeable world.

"A pleasant day for a walk," said Frank, as he passed him with a friendly nod.

The man looked up, and fixed his eyes on the speaker in a long, rude stare. This was by no means the first time he had been spoken to by a Hall-boy, for the wilder spirits of the school had been often led into serious mischief by Ed Bailey and his comrades; but this was one of the "Snobs," — as the loungers at Milward's Corner had nicknamed those of the school-boys who held themselves above such low companionship, — and the "Snobs" never deigned even a look to him and his friends.

"I feel as if I could almost walk up to your beautiful home at Mountain Lake, Bailey," Frank went on, returning his stare with a smile. "This cool, fresh air braces one up so."

The man gave him a quick, sharp look as

if to ask whether there were any motive for those words other than appeared on the surface; but Austin met his glance frankly, and forced, as it seemed, it spite of himself to make some reply, Bailey answered, gruffly, —

"It's good enough, I suppose."

"We were up there a day or two since," said Frank, unabashed by his disagreeable manner. "The country was looking splendidly, and the lake was as clear as crystal. We were fortunate in finding it so perfectly clear, for I believe the water is sometimes a little muddied, isn't it?"

"Summat so," was all the answer he received.

But no matter, Frank had something to do, and he meant to do it.

"One of our ladies fell into the lake. She wasn't hurt at all; and your mother gave her dry clothes, and made her as comfortable as possible. If Mrs. Bailey had been her own mother, she couldn't have been more kind and attentive to her. She's a very nice old lady. We all liked her so much."

The keen, black eyes had fixed themselves on Frank's face at the first mention of the mother. Frank knew that very well, but he had not lifted his to meet them. Now, looking up suddenly, he caught their expression,— a softened look which Edward Bailey would never willingly have permitted him to see. It changed in an instant to the old sullen, moody expression; but the boy had seen it, and it was all he needed to confirm him in his purpose.

Wisely thinking that his first effort had been carried far enough, he turned into a foot-path, which led across the fields up to the Hall, saying, as he left his strange companion,—

"I must hurry, or I shall be late. Good-morning."

"Mornin'," was the roughly spoken response.

But the next moment, with a quick spring, the man had gained Frank's side once more.

"I say," he said, without looking toward Austin, but keeping close beside him, "the old woman didn't happen to say nothin' to you about me, did she now?"

"No, not to me," replied Frank. "But she told one of the ladies that she had a son in Graydon who had not visited her in a long while, and that she wanted very much indeed to see him."

The words were scarcely spoken before his listener was gone, and Frank walked rapidly on toward the Hall.

Had he found the soft spot in that hard heart? Had he seen the glow of a diamond hidden deep, deep down beneath a crushing weight of sin and folly and ignorance?

It was a morning in the middle of September, and the mellow autumn light was beginning to fall softly over hill and valley, tinting the already rich landscape with even brighter hues. The varied bits of color caught Austin's eye, and he stood for a moment watching the changes in the beautiful picture with keen delight.

In the valley at his feet lay a smooth meadow of bright green, stretching away toward the hills, until it was met by a field of red buckwheat lying cosily nestled between two fields of corn that stood proudly tossing its long tassels in the sunlight, even while it bent beneath the weight of its golden ears. Here and there over the meadows the maples waved their branches in the breeze, some tipped with yellow or crimson leaves, or touched in the very heart with scarlet hues, while the outer branches still wore their early dress of green. Away up on the mountain side there shone a gleam of purest white, — a late field, which the sun, lingering in the valley, coquetting with waving corn and sweet blossoms there, had neglected to care for. It would scarcely ripen now, yet it added another shade to the picture. Father down the hillside a broad, brown expanse, bringing out the brighter colors in stronger relief, told that the ploughman had been busy there. Barren enough it looked as his eye first fell on it; but the next moment, the sunlight touching it from behind a passing cloud, clothed it with a new beauty, bringing into view a faint shade of softest green, the first tender up-springing of the winter grain which needed that one burst of sunshine to tell that it was there.

So it is oftentimes with poor human souls. We pass them by, for they seem to us utterly barren, rough, and dark. But let the sunshine of a gentle word, a generous act, or even a kindly smile but fall upon them, and we shall catch in a moment the answering gleam, the quick up-springing of a new life. It may be but a germ, so slight and faint that we shall lose it as the shadow falls again; yet, if it is tended and cared for, it will, in God's good time, bear fruit which we shall gather into His treasure-house, singing our Harvest-Home with glad thanksgiving.

IV

MILWARD'S CORNER.

THE Sabbath morning rose bright and and fair after two days of heavy rain; and as Frank Austin sat in the little Graydon Church, by a window which looked out upon a brook whose waters had been swollen into quite a sturdy stream by the storm, the glorious sunlight which bathed the whole scene in gold seemed to him a promise of success in the work which he intended to begin that afternoon. The sun-lit water came gurgling and splashing over the stones which lay in its path until, striking a sharp ledge of rock, it dashed over its edge in a miniature waterfall, which fell foaming into a deep pool that lay dark and silent beneath the rock.

Watching the glistening water as it fell, the boy's thoughts wandered far out of the reach of Mr. Leonard's voice. The dark, deep pool was Milward's Corner; the sparkling, flashing stream which threw itself into it, fearless of stain from contact with its blackness, was the feeble band who had undertaken to labor for the Master there.

But what was this lying just beyond the spot where the bright water struck the dark?

A tiny leaf, lifted by some playful breeze from an autumn-tinted maple-bough, lay burning on the black water; now floating out toward a broad land of sunlight which lay warmly across the brook not half a dozen feet from it; now drawn back by the current of the pool; now thrown forward again by the onward force of the little cataract. That tiny leaf grew to a sign to the boy; it took upon it a strange importance, an individuality, it became his "rough diamond." Would the deep pool draw it down, down to its dark depths, or would the pure, sweet stream move it on little by little to the bright sunlight beyond?

He sat and watched and watched it with a curious, almost painful earnestness. Back and forth, back and forth, first subject to one force, then to the other; but with all its turnings and waverings, Frank could see that it was slowly floating toward the light. A trifle nearer, another trifle, and then a slight breeze ruffled the stream, and wafted the glowing leaf, the bearer of so many hopes and longings, into the glorious, shining band of gold which spanned the stream.

Frank lifted his head with a great sigh of relief. A half-smile crossed his face as he became conscious of the depth and intensity of feeling with which he had followed the fate of a little maple-leaf; and, looking up with the smile yet on his lips, he caught Mr. Leonard's eyes fixed full upon his face, with something so like an answering gleam in their quiet depths, that the boy asked himself if it could be that he too had seen the pretty, trifling thing, and had invested it with any such importance as that which he had attached to it. But that could not be; for, from his position, Mr. Leonard could by no possibility have looked out upon the little picture. For a moment, Frank wondered what that glance had meant; then something in the sermon caught his wandering thoughts, and the circumstance passed from his mind.

He was standing in the vestibule of the church after service, talking with Christy, who had stopped him on his way out, to ask him some question with reference to the meeting at the Corner, when Mr. Leonard came down the aisle, and pausing beside them, said: —

"Well, Frank, are you ready to open the battle this afternoon?"

"Yes, sir, I believe so. Christy and I were just discussing the matter a little. I've one good helper, at any rate."

"Yes; and you would have more if I did not think it wisest — at least for the present — to leave the field entirely in your hands. All my own efforts have been so resolutely and bitterly withstood, that I have been almost in despair of any good being done at the Corner while Milward kept up his tavern there; the very word "minister" or "church" seems to be sufficient to excite the opposition of those poor creatures; but since you boys have undertaken the work, I have some hope in it. There will be the novelty of the thing, in the first place, to attract them, and the more hardened of them will not think it worth their while to interfere with what they will probably consider mere child's play. They will laugh at you, mock you, and annoy you, doubtless, in every way possible to their ingenuity; but they will scarcely oppose you with any thing like violence; and they will soon tire of their system of annoyance, I think, and leave you to go on your way unmolested.

You have undertaken a noble work, my son. God bless you in it!"

Christy left them at the church-door, promising to be in his place at the appointed time; and Mr. Leonard and Frank were slowly walking homeward, when the minister asked, suddenly, —

"What was your text this morning, Frank?"

"The text, sir?" and Frank colored slightly, for, for the moment, it had escaped him. "Oh! I have it now. 'I am the good shepherd and know my sheep, and am known of mine.'"

"That was my text: I asked you for yours. You heard but little of my sermon this morning; but if I am not much mistaken you heard a greater preacher than I. Was not that so?"

The boy looked up, with a quick, comprehending glance.

"I know what you mean," he said, "and I know, too, why it was that you looked as if you saw the picture which had drawn my attention from your sermon. Did you see it, Mr. Leonard?"

"I saw a face in which watchfulness and anxiety, hope, uncertainty, and strong desire were strangely mixed and blended; then I saw the watchful anxiety subside into almost certain hope, then into fulfilled desire, and I knew that my young soldier had been armed anew, and that his Captain had strengthened him for the battle. You need not have blushed to find that you were not at once able to give me my text when you supposed that I had asked for it, for I think you have been listening to Him who preached to the fishermen of Galilee. Can you tell me His text?"

"A little maple-leaf, tossed to and fro, but lifted at last into the sunny, quiet water," said Frank, smiling. "That was the text, and the sermon has made me strong for my work. But I had not thought of it so before. You always have such a nice way of putting things, Mr. Leonard;" and he drew closer to the minister's side, and looked lovingly up in his face.

"Have I, my boy?" he answered, gravely. "I am glad if I have helped you in any degree. Since Allan Haywood, your friend and my son (as dear to me as my very own, though he called another man father) went home, the young friends he left behind him, especially those who love and serve the Master whom he so delighted to honor, stand next to him in my love; and I would fain do for them what, if God had spared his life, I might have done for him. Remember, Frank, that if at any time you want my aid, I am always more than ready, both with hand and heart."

"I know that, sir, and I shall never forget it," said Frank; and their paths diverging here, they parted with a hearty grasp of each other's hands, and another wish from Mr. Leonard that the boy might prosper in his new enterprise.

Mrs. Tracy's apartment was a small corner room, on the second floor of a dilapidated wooden building which stood close beside the tavern, where, for years, Joe Milward had doled out disease and death, at three cents a glass, to scores and hundreds of poor souls who flocked day by day to his den of misery. Young men and old, women, and even children, might be seen at any hour of the day, idling about the ill-kept, tumble-down tavern, hanging around the door in groups, or issuing from the bar, staggering stupidly under the influence of the poison they had taken; or, maddened by its heat, raving like lunatics, until, worn out by their own violence, they fell down, a helpless heap of rags and wretchedness, into heavy, senseless sleep.

A few benches had been placed in rows along one side of the room, fronting an old school-desk which Dr. Drayton had given to be used as a rostrum; the broken boards of the bare floor had been covered here and there by patches of bright carpet obtained from Mrs. Morton, the housekeeper; and the two small windows had been neatly curtained with coarse white muslin. Altogether it was by no means an uninviting looking spot; and as Frank, with half a dozen of his schoolfellows, entered it that sunny September afternoon, he thought it, in his glad, hopeful enthusiasm, the very place for a prayer-meeting such as he designed to hold.

"Surely they will come in," he said to himself, as he glanced around the room; "it looks so neat and cosy they will like it."

And they did come in. First of all — save Christy and his two boys, who were waiting at the door when Frank reached the Corner — came two or three children; then a group of boys about his own age; ten or twelve of these, rough, ill-looking young fellows; then an old woman; then a girl, with a baby in her arms; and then, sauntering slowly in, as if half undecided whether to enter the room or not, — Ed Bailey.

Frank had just risen, to open the service, when the last comer loitered lazily through the open door. Austin paused a moment, with the eyes of all the little crowd upon him, until Bailey was fairly in the room; then said, quietly,—

"Will you please to close that door, and we will begin our service."

The young man stood still for a moment, eyeing him sharply; then, as if suddenly changing his mind, turned and shut the door, seating himself close beside it.

It was a moment of intense interest to every one within the walls of that poor room. Whatever motive had brought them there, however carelessly or with whatever evil intent they had come, every faculty of every soul there was now engrossed by that young face behind the desk. Idle curiosity had drawn the two women,— the rumor of some kind of a meeting to be held in the Widow Tracy's room. At the tavern it had been talked of, too; in the bar-room some one had said that the "Snobs were goin' to get up a meetin'." The announcement had been simply laughed at save by Milward, who had declared with a curse that, "if the young rascals" interfered with him, they would make trouble for themselves. The love of something new, and the hope of making some fun, had drawn a number of the frequenters of the bar from their usual Sunday afternoon recreations to the little room; but there was not one stranger there who had come to worship God. Nevertheless, the room was solemnly still, and every eye was fixed on Frank, as he faced the small company who sat before him, wondering how much he had courage to do and say.

They had not long to wait. He was very pale, but his voice came full and clear and strong when, after a moment's pause, it broke the silence: —

"We are very glad, more glad than we

can tell you, to see so many here, especially so many young fellows of about our own age. We boys thought it would be a good idea, as long as there was no church in this part of the village, to hold a meeting here,—a sociable, friendly kind of an affair. Sunday is such a long, dull day when we have nothing at all to do and don't go to church, that any thing that breaks into it, and gives us something to think of and talk about, is a very good thing for us. So we thought we would start this meeting, and those that liked it could come, and those that did not need not be at all annoyed by it, as we are quite out of the way. It is a real satisfaction to us to see so many here. We scarcely expected it, and it is a great encouragement. We will begin, by singing the hymn on the sixth page of those little books which you will see on the benches."

Two or three hands were stretched out for the books; and three voices, one that of the girl with the baby on her knees, joined in, as Will Seaton, — who had come down " to see the fun " as he expressed it, but in reality to help Frank out of his difficulty with regard to a chorister, — struck up the old familiar tune of " America," to the hymn, —

" Come, thou Almighty King."

Frank had but little ear for music, and could not have carried a tune if his life depended on it; but he listened with infinite delight to the hymn, nor did it disturb his happiness when he noticed that one of the two strangers, who lent their voices to the chorus, was singing the words as well as the tune of " America." The man had not opened a book, but sat with his hands in his pocket, and his head thrown back, singing away most lustily, in a voice by no means unmelodious, — bringing his feet down with a smart rap upon the floor at the close of every line, not apparently with any idea of making a disturbance, but simply in his full content and enjoyment.

Little by little others began to sing, until at last there was scarcely one in the room who sat silent and seemingly uninterested except Edward Bailey. Since he had seated himself beside the door he had not raised his head, nor taken any notice of any one around him, except to push aside with a gruff refusal a hymn-book which Laurence Bronson had offered him.

The notes of the hymn died down into silence; there was a moment's pause, and then Frank rose in his place again.

"We have asked God to help us to sing," he said, looking round as he spoke on the group about him, with a face that showed he felt some doubt as to the spirit in which his words would be received, but speaking in a firm, decided tone; "Let us ask Him to bless us with His love."

"No! no! none of that, youngster," said

a voice from the farther side of the room. "Sing as much as you like; but we ain't a goin' to have no prayin' here."

"No, not a bit of it!" shouted another voice; and cries of, "No! no!" "No prayin' here!" "No preachin' in these parts!" and so forth, were shouted in a tumultuous chorus, which effectually prevented any efforts on Frank's part to make himself heard.

He did not attempt to speak, but stood in his place, very pale; looking from one to another of the more violent of his opposers, until his very stillness silenced them. The uproar died into a murmur of discontent, — then ceased entirely, every one watching to see what the next move would be. No sooner had the room become quite still than Austin spoke.

"I should be sorry," he said quietly, "to do any thing which would annoy any one here; but all, who have come into this room, came probably with the full knowledge that the meeting in which they intended to take part was to be held for the service of God. It must be remembered that this room is, for the time being, my house. I am very glad to welcome you all to it, but those of us who are here to serve our Lord and Master must not be disturbed. If any wish to leave before prayer is offered, they may do so at once."

There was a moment's pause, but no one moved.

"Look a here, Snobby!" said the man who had first interrupted the service, a rough, burly fellow, who had come in for the express purpose of defeating the object of the meeting, "if you think you're a goin' to settle down in this place and play missionary, you're just mistaken, and the sooner you stop this, the better for you;" and rising from his seat, he stood with his hands in his pockets, eying Frank with an impudent stare.

"Go it, Bill!" "Two to one on big Bill!" "No, I'll bet on Snobby; he's got the real grit!" and so forth, were some of the cries which rang through the room; while the smaller boys clapped their hands, whistled, and shouted their approval of the turn affairs were taking.

Frank did not speak, but his steady eye never moved from the face of the man who defied him, until the din and noise subsided again; then he said, —

"I must have quiet here. No one has a right to interfere with us in our own room."

"No more they haven't," exclaimed the man who had sung so heartily, starting suddenly to his feet. "Sit down, Bill Simpson, and give the young 'un fair play. He's on his own floor; and if he's a likin' for prayin', 'tain't none of our consarns. Them's as don't like it here can go where they're better suited. Come now, fellers, sit down, and let him go ahead. The sooner he gits through, the sooner we'll git to singin' agin, and I'm just full of sing. Go ahead, young Snobby! I'll see you git fair play."

But the opposition was not to be so soon silenced; and the tumult, especially among the smaller boys, was fast rising again, when from the door-way there came another voice to the rescue, — a voice by no means as persuasive as that of Frank's first friend, but far more potent in its effect.

"Sit down, and stay down, every mother's son of you, or I'll know the reason why!" it said fiercely; and the boys sat down with a celerity that astonished the speaker himself.

The burly man in the corner still maintained his ground, looking round defiantly, but said nothing further. Frank glanced round to see who his new champion might be, and great was his surprise to find that it was Edward Bailey.

The room was as still now as if there were no living soul within it but himself; all were watching to see whether he would dare to begin his prayer. There was an instant's silence; then a low, quiet voice broke it so gently, that all had to listen intently if they wished to know for what it plead.

And it did plead. It asked for very little: only for the light of God's love to cheer and comfort each heart there; for daily health and strength to win what the daily needs of each required; for peace and joy and rest to be given to each; for very little, counting by words and by the minutes during which the low, earnest voice held the rough crowd silent; but for good which was beyond all measure if one judged by those tones of longing entreaty.

Not one head was bent save those of his own friends; but when Austin lifted his face again and turned to his little audience, he found every eye fixed upon him, not in malice or mischief, but in interest and admiration. Not that his prayer, simple and earnest though it was, had reached those poor, hardened souls; but boys, even the worst of them, have always a spot in their hearts which any exhibition of true courage will touch; and they had seen in this boy, no older than many of themselves, a moral fortitude and bravery which had kindled into light every spark of honor which yet smouldered in their breasts. Not a disturbing sound was heard, as Frank again spoke.

"I see some one with us," he said, looking over toward the corner from which Christy and his two sons had been anxiously watching the progress of affairs, "from whom we would all be glad to hear; for he is the friend, I suppose, of every man, woman, and child here. We will sing another hymn, and then we will ask Mr. Dunn to talk to us a little."

The hymn was sung; and then the old man left his seat, and coming forward stepped behind the desk, Frank having motioned to him to take his place.

"I've just a bit of a story to tell you," he

said, as he leaned forward on the desk, " of a poor young fellow that got into sore mishaps. His father was a rich man and a good man too; and he'd a great love for this boy and for another son he had, an older one. The older one was a good lad, but this younger boy was of a restless, rovin' mind, and he got into evil ways, and fell from bad to worse, till at last he wouldn't even live in the house with his father and the rest of the family; for he felt uneasy in his conscience, and, I suppose, couldn't bear to see the odds betwixt himself and them, they being good and honest folks, and he bein' of a very different turn of mind. So he takes his share of what fortune the old man had to give, and off he goes to furrin' parts. Just think of the meanness of it, boys, to take the money that the poor old man had been layin' up for years, and instead of helpin' along in the family, to go off with it as if he'd earned it all himself.

" Well, for years they didn't see him, only

heard of him from time to time, and every time a worse tale. The old father's heart was a'most broke with shame and grief; for his honest name was dragged in the dirt, his money squandered, and his boy lost to him.

"By and by, one day, as his weary eyes was a lookin' out upon the road, he sees a figure, all rags and misery, bent and broken-like, a comin' up the road. He looks at it, and as he looks he gets all of a tremble. He thinks he knows it. Poor and ragged and forlorn as it is, he thinks it is his son. He looks again, his breath comes thick and fast, and he moves — not to the door to enter in and lock it fast against his wicked son. No, my boys, no: it is to run and meet him, to take him in his old arms, to kiss his poor, wan face, old before its time; and as the son, penitent and heart-broken, sobs out so humble-like, 'Father, I have sinned!' the father but holds him closer, and cries out so joyful that all run to see what has cheered his sad heart so greatly. Never a word of anger falls from his lips; the son had but to say he was sorry, and the father forgave it all and took him to his home and his heart again. So God, our Father, will take us in tender, loving forgiveness, so soon as we turn back from our sinful ways, and do but whisper,— 'Father, I have sinned!'"

"Please dismiss them, Christy," whispered Frank, as the old man left the desk.

He did not return to his place; but from where he stood, lifting his wrinkled hands, he said simply,—

"Dear Father! win us back to Thee from all our wanderings and sin. Lead us now from this place, guiding us to our homes with the light of Thy blessing."

The little assemblage broke up quietly; and so ended Frank's first effort at Milward's Corner.

V.

MARY ALLEN.

"WELL, Austin, what do you think of that?" asked Will Seaton, as the school-boys set off together toward the Hall after the meeting had broken up.

"I think that was pretty well for a beginning," replied Frank; "did you imagine they would let us go to work so peaceably? I fully expected a disturbance."

"A disturbance! Well, I'd like to know what you call that small interruption by the gentleman in the red shirt, if it wasn't a disturbance. What did you expect? A cannonade of doubtful eggs and fish-tails?"

"I shouldn't have been a bit surprised if we had been saluted in some such way," said Frank, seriously. "You don't suppose, Will, that those people are going to let us do all we can to spoil their trade without trying to stop us, do you? I'm very thankful that we've had such a quiet time to-day; but I don't believe we've seen the worst of our experience yet, even if we did have to fight pretty hard for a hearing. They won't let us draw away their custom without a battle."

"Then you still have some hopes on the rotten eggs and so forth question, have you?" and Seaton laughed merrily. "Wouldn't you have looked jolly if one had struck you square on the forehead, or in the mouth, just as you began to speak! Wouldn't I have roared!"

"No, you wouldn't," said Frank, smiling. "You would have looked as grave and serious as you did all through the service this afternoon. I must thank all you fellows for standing by me as you did; you were just splendid to keep your seats and hold your tongues all through that uproar. As for you,

Will, I surely expected you would pitch in. I didn't think you could sit so still in a scrimmage."

"I didn't know it myself. In fact, I thought every minute I'd be out of my seat when that big fellow was blowing away so, and those little rascals were larking it on the back seats. Didn't I want to jump over the benches and settle those youngsters, though? But you looked so well able to look after your own pie, that I thought I'd better not put my fingers in it. Besides, I had a small dose of caution before I left the Hall. Prof. called me into the lecture-room after we came home from church, and told me he'd heard you depended on me to attend to the musical part of the affair; that, in fact, I was to be the star of the occasion, and he hoped I'd shine."

"O Will, what a whopper!"

"'Tisn't a whopper, either. He said just that,— not in those very words, of course; you know Prof. and I never do express ourselves in exactly the same terms. For instance, if I were describing you, I'd say you were up to snuff and pretty spicy; rather high in the instep, perhaps, but, after all, just as jolly a good fellow as I know, and pretty good-looking to boot. But if Prof. had you in hand, he'd introduce you as — 'Mr. Francis Austin, gentlemen: a young person who is entirely conversant with the leading events of the times, of keen perceptions and decided action; rather inclined to a proud and dignified bearing, perhaps; but, after all, a young gentleman of pleasant social qualities, and of the highest culture; adding to these mental endowments the attractions of a well-proportioned and manly form, and a face of refined and intellectual beauty.' How's that?" and he glanced mischievously round at his companions.

"First rate! Prof. to a T!" said Laurence Bronson, as the whole group burst into a hearty laugh at the close of Will's description.

"Take care, boys," said Frank. "We ought not to make such a noise in the road. That wasn't bad, Will; but we mustn't forget it's Sunday."

"But what did he really say to you, Seaton?" asked Charlie Grant, one of the younger boys of the school, a timid little fellow, who stood in such awe of Dr. Drayton that he scarcely dared to laugh at fun made at his expense, even when at the distance of nearly two miles from the Hall. "I shouldn't have thought he'd let you come at all," he added, innocently.

"Holloa! small boy, what do you mean by that? Do you want a shaking?" and, seizing the child as if he meant to make good his threat, Seaton tossed him up on his shoulder, and pursued his way up the hill as if the extra sixty-five or seventy pounds' weight he carried were rather a help than otherwise in his upward journey.

"What did he say?" he repeated, when

the child was safely perched on his throne, "really, I can't tell you. Ask him yourself when we get to the Hall. He's always ready to inform the inquiring mind on any subject. Shall I tell him that you'd like to see him?"

"No, I thank you," said Charlie, laughing, and giving Will's tawny locks a sly pull. "I'll wait a while before I ask the doctor, I think."

Will's answer, "I can't tell you," needed to be taken in the sense rather of "I will not" than "I cannot," for not one word of the doctor's caution had he forgotten. To tell the truth, Dr. Drayton had been very much inclined to say at once, when Austin told him he had accepted Seaton's good-humored offer to lead the singing for him, that he could not consent to any such arrangement. But when he said as much to Frank, he had seemed so confident that Seaton's goodness of heart would control his love of fun, and that he would be hurt and mortified by a refusal of his services, that the doctor had contented himself with giving him a warning, not only to be quiet and decorous, but also with regard to interfering impetuously in any difficulty which might arise between Austin and the Milward's Corner division of the company.

"Bronson will be there," he had said, "and old Christy, to lend Austin whatever aid he may require. They can conduct an argument with calmness; but if trouble arises and you attempt to interfere, it will be simply impossible for you to do so with coolness and moderation. You will only harm him; and that, I am sure, you would be very sorry to do."

"I would so," said Seaton, bluntly. "I wouldn't do that for the world; for I tell you, Dr. Drayton, it takes a pretty plucky chap to undertake such a business as this. I'd be as sorry as anybody if things should go against him."

"I know that, Seaton," said the doctor. "I am glad and thankful that you feel inclined to lend Austin your countenance and encouragement in this matter; it will do him good; it has done him good already; but I sincerely hope that you will content yourself with simply giving him the aid of your voice. Let that be raised in all its sweetness and beauty when he asks for it, for God has blessed you with a noble gift which He has denied to Frank; but let it be raised *only* when he asks for it. It is the sweetest, clearest voice I know," he added, looking kindly at the boy, " when it is used in song; but it is too strong and impetuous, too hot and fiery in discussion, to be a safe voice to plead Austin's cause; as I know that it will long to do if there is any difficulty with those people. Promise me, Seaton, that you will not allow yourself to be led into argument."

" Very well, sir," said Will, looking half-pleased and half-amused. " But if they do get into a muss, I'll have to walk out. I couldn't stand by and see those fellows pitching into Frank without giving them the benefit of my views; so I'll just have to come away. But I guess we'll get along all right."

"I hope so," said the doctor, with his queer, grim smile.

Then Seaton had left him, saying to himself as he closed the study-door, "I declare! the old Prof. would be quite a brick if one could only get a little of the starch out of him. I do believe he really loves Austin. And that wasn't bad he said about my voice, either. Well, well; it's a good thing, Will, my boy, that he sees one thing in you that's sweet, for he thinks that on most points you're sour enough to make a fellow's eyes jump out of his head."

But in spite of all his folly, the boy had been touched and pleased by the master's kindly words and look, although he would not have confessed it for a kingdom.

Meanwhile, at the Corner, the little prayer-meeting was discussed with no less animation and interest. As the loungers sauntered into the bar-room, or hung about the door of the tavern, each had some mocking, sneering question to ask of those who had spent the last hour in Mrs. Tracy's room.

"There wasn't half as much fun as we thought there'd be," said one of the boys who had attempted to bear Simpson out in his opposition. "The fellers let Snobby browbeat 'em. And then Ed Bailey, he went over to their side when we tried to make a muss. Are you a goin' to be a Methody, Ed?" he added, turning toward Bailey, who was leaning against the door.

"No: I ain't goin' to do nothin' of the sort," answered Bailey, gruffly; "but I like fair play, and I'll see it, too, even on the side of the Snobs. We ain't got no business to go into his room and get up a row. If we don't like his doin's we can stay out. He's got a right to his own premises."

"I guess he thinks so," said another young fellow who stood near. "He looked like he did when he stood behind that ere desk, eyin' of us all when we was hallooin' and whistlin'. He's a pretty lively kind of a chap, too; he ain't none of your snivellin', cantin' sort, but he'll do what he sets out to, if it costs him all he's got. You'd better look out for him, Milward."

"He'd better look out for himself," returned the bar-keeper, whose temper had been exceedingly disturbed by the fact of Bailey's having taken part with the new-comers against his friends and supporters. "If he meddles with me or my business it'll be the worse for him. He'd better try it."

"And you'd better let him alone if you know what's good for yourself," replied Bailey, sullenly. "The place is his own, and if he's meddled with his people are ready to look after him, I guess; and it'll be about as good for us not to have 'em peerin' too close into our affairs, Milward. Give me a glass o' Jamaica."

He tossed some money down on the counter as he spoke, and Milward bustled about to prepare what he had asked for. Bailey was too influential a person among his customers for him to offend him lightly; and it was in quite an altered tone that he answered, as he set the glass down before him, —

"No offence, Ed; but a feller don't like to be interfered with. I don't mean no harm to the chap, 'specially if you've taken a likin' to him."

"I ain't taken no likin' to him," returned Bailey, fiercely, quite unmollified by his friend's suavity. "What's he to me, I'd like to know? But I won't see nobody nor nothin', not even a dog, run down unfair. What's the Snobs to us, anyhow? Let them go their gait, and we'll go our own. Come on, boys, I'll treat all round."

Whatever ailed Bailey that afternoon, it did not seem to be any leaning toward the change of feeling with which one of his companions had charged him. Not a man of all the company was more loud and boisterous than he; none drank deeper, nor played more desperately.

"Look a here, Milward," said one of his customers, as the tavern-keeper, late in the evening, returned to the bar from which he had been absent a short time, "Ed don't look very Methody just now."

"Oh! I guess he's all right," answered the man, with a coarse laugh, as he glanced at Bailey's prostrate form stretched upon the floor in a heavy stupor. "I ain't much afraid they'll catch him. He always had ridikerlous kind of notions about stickin' up for the weak side of a fight, that's all. Them pious folks'll never come it over him. He's safe to lie here this way every night that he's got money in his pocket."

As the man spoke, a figure rose from a chair at the farther side of the room, and came slowly forward. It was the girl with the baby. She held it still; it lay asleep in her arms as she walked slowly across the floor, passing among the miserable forms which lay upon the dirty boards, or sat sunk in a heap upon the chairs around the table in the centre of the room, with a look of aversion and repugnance on her thin face.

"Why, Mollie, is that you?" said Milward, as she came near him. "I didn't know you was back there."

"I was chill, and came in to get warm,— me and baby."

The words were spoken in a dull, heavy tone; but the listless voice took an accent of tenderness as those two little syllables left her lips, and the weary eyes looked lovingly down at the small bundle in her arms.

"What's the matter, girl? You're down to-night."

"Not down so far as that," she said, touching Bailey's motionless figure with her foot.

"No," answered the man, with a laugh. "But you're pale and cold, Mollie. Come along, and I'll give you a glass to warm you up. What makes you look so? You're enough to frighten the little chap, if he wakes and looks at you."

"It's just him as makes me look so," returned the girl, fixing her eyes on Milward's face. "I'm thinking that that's the way he'll lie maybe, one of these days, if you live long enough to tempt him. That is, if he has money in his pocket," she added, with a sneer.

The man looked at her in silent amazement for a moment; then he said, almost timidly,— "Why, Mollie girl, what's come to you?"

"I don't know," she answered. "I don't know at all what's come to me; but I know I hate this place, and I hate you, Joe Milward, and I hate this low, wicked life worse than either. And I know one thing more; and that is, that my little child (and that sweet thrill rang through her voice again), my little child shall be saved from it if his mother can save him. You took away my husband and his father from me; but you shall not take his mother from him too, for I will never set my foot in this wretched den again;" and passing him with a quick step she went out into the night, leaving Milward standing looking after her, too much astonished to answer.

"Well," he said at last, "if it don't beat all. She's taken a pretty sudden turn."

It was not to be wondered at that the man could scarcely believe his own senses. Three years before, Mary Allen's parents, both in Milward's employ, and both the victims of his miserable traffic, had died, leaving her in his house friendless and alone; and he had allowed her to remain there in return for such services as she could render.

Two years ago this Sabbath night, she had married a young man whom Milward had just engaged as bar-tender. Scarcely a month had passed, when she found that her young husband was falling under the influence of the landlord and his friends; and eighteen months afterwards, he was killed in a drunken quarrel in the tavern. Only eighteen years of age, with a little baby a few weeks old to be cared for, the poor girl knew no other home to which to turn; and she had lived on in the wretched place ever since, a miserable, hopeless life, but a life from which she seemed to have no energy nor even a desire to escape. It was no marvel that Milward, accustomed to seeing her pass listlessly to and fro, apparently unmoved by any of the scenes which were daily enacted before her, should be utterly surprised and confounded by her sudden attack upon him.

Mollie had walked rapidly up the main street of the village for some distance, and then turning sharply from it into a narrower road, had begun to ascend the long hill toward Drayton Hall. She had gone on for part of the way, when, suddenly pausing, she began to look about her as if not quite certain where she was going.

"Why, what am I about?" she said, at

length, putting her hand to her head as if she were dazed. "I'm on the Hall road;" and turning, she began slowly to retrace her steps.

"Where shall I go?" she said to herself, when she had walked back some distance toward the village again. "He mustn't be out here much longer. It's growing so cold and sharp;" and taking off the thin shawl which covered her shoulders, she wrapped it about the child who still slept peacefully in her arms.

By and by she passed a deserted barn. She paused a moment, as if half inclined to enter; but changing her mind, went on again, walking very fast to keep herself warm, for she was only half-clad, and the night was damp and chilly.

But after a while her steps began to lag; she was growing very weary, and there was no place of shelter anywhere within sight.

"I must have come round by some wrong path," she said to herself. "Where am I, I wonder? Oh, deary me! I'm on the mountain road, and there's never a house nor a barn anywhere near this. I'll have to go back."

With a sigh, she turned again on her steps. The baby stirred with a fretful cry. She rocked him gently to and fro, whispering softly, —

"Don't cry, sweet, don't. Mother can't bear it just now. We'll find a roof to cover us soon. But I can't go back to that hole. Never, never!"

When he was quiet again she went on, and after a while reached the old barn which she had passed before. She did not hesitate now, but going directly in, was about to seat herself on a dark object near the shattered doorway, when the thing moved; and starting up with a cry, she found that what she had taken in the darkness for the trunk of a tree, was a cow. The animal rose, and walked slowly out.

"She must have left a warm spot there,

baby dear," whispered the young mother. "We'll lie down where she lay."

It was a hard bed, with not even a billet of wood for a pillow; but the girl was exhausted with her long walk, and scarcely had her head touched the floor before she fell asleep. A troubled sleep at first, broken by dreams of Milward, who seemed to be dragging her baby from her; then of Austin and old Christy; but by and by she lay quiet and still, the baby clasped close to her breast.

VI.

IN THE OLD BARN.

IT was long after sunrise on the morning of the next day, when Mary Allen, disturbed by the fretful wailing of her baby, woke from the heavy sleep into which she had fallen. An indistinct consciousness that the child had been crying for a long while was floating dimly through her mind, but she did not seem able to exert herself to tend it. She lay, with her eyes half-closed, listening to its moans with a vague idea that it needed something, and that she ought to rouse herself; yet with such an utter lack of energy both of body and mind, that the mere effort to turn her head to look at her child was greater than she seemed able to make.

But after a while the fretful wail changed to a sharper cry; and, with a startled, frightened sort of feeling, the girl tried to raise herself. Tried in vain at first, sinking weakly back upon the floor when she had scarcely more than lifted her head from the hard boards.

"Given out at last," she said. "I wondered how soon it would come. I suppose I'll never get up."

The words were spoken in a dull, listless tone, as if it mattered nothing to her whether she ever rose or not; and she lay quiet once more until the baby's sharp cry roused her again. She opened her eyes, and looked at him for a moment, almost stupidly; and then, suddenly, as if the conviction had just flashed upon her, she said, —

"Can he be hungry? Oh, yes, it's morning. He must be hungry."

She tried again to rise; but failing, and finding the baby in her weakness too great a burden for her, laid him down upon the floor; and then, struggling up upon her hands and knees, crept across the boards to an old hay-rick, and, holding fast to it, at length managed to stand upon her feet. Her head swam dizzily with the effort, and she staggered back feebly against the uncertain support. Her mouth was dry, and burning with fever; and feeling as if she must have water, she picked up a rusty tin cup which lay on the floor near her, and clinging to the wall crept to the doorway. She looked out, hoping to see some little spring of water, or even a puddle by the roadside, where she might cool her parched lips; but it was all as dry as the boards beneath her feet. She was turning back, when the cow which she had disturbed the night before came slowly round from the other side of the barn.

"I wonder if I could milk her," said the girl. "Only I'm feared to let go the door, lest I fall. So, bossy, so!" and she looked entreatingly at the creature as she drew nearer, as if she could comprehend her words, and help her in her great need. "You've been milked already, poor thing; but baby is starving, and I'll die of thirst."

The animal stood still as if she had understood every word she said. Perhaps she was won by the low, pitiful voice. At any rate she paused close beside the door-way; and sinking down upon the sill, Mary tried to fill the old cup. At first, her weak fingers refused to aid her; but after a little they seemed to gain some strength, and by and by the cup was filled with rich, foaming milk. She put it to her lips; and refreshed and strengthened, at least for the moment, crept back to the spot where her baby lay, still wailing feebly, for his louder cry had been but momentary.

She took him in her lap; he was not much to hold, — poor little thing. He had always looked as if a fresh breeze might waft him away some sunny morning; now, as he lay with closed eyes upon her knees, quieted for a moment by the touch of her tender hands, the tiny, colorless face was absolutely lifeless in its expression. And, after all, he would take but little of the hardly earned breakfast. What he did take, however, served to still his cries, and he fell asleep on his mother's lap. Mary sat looking down at him for a while; and then her own eyelids began to droop, and resting her child on her arm she lay back upon the floor.

But she did not sleep. Her mind wandered back to the past day; not to its last miserable occurrences in Milward's bar-room, but to that little service in Mrs. Tracy's room. All its scenes passed before her as if they were actually enacted again. She heard the rich, sweet voice lifting the words of the gladsome hymn, joined after the first moment by others, voices which she had never known to speak a holy word before. She heard the pleasant words of welcome; then she saw a pale, resolute face, glowing with earnest desire, as, the short conflict over, the young leader sought help and comfort and strength for the needy hearts around him; and then that other face, with its crown of silver hair, looking so tenderly round upon them all, while the old, faded lips told the story of the sorrowful, penitent child's loving reception at his father's home. She smiled as it came up before her, and the smile deepened and brightened as that picture floated by to give place to another, — the face of the boy behind the desk who had seemed to know so well what she wanted, and how tried and troubled she had been, and to be so ready and so anxious to ask God to help her. And then the words of the second hymn came softly through the air: —

> "Just as I am, — without one plea,
> But that thy blood was shed for me,
> And that Thou bids't me come to Thee, —
> O Lamb of God! I come.

"Just as I am, — and waiting not
To rid my soul of one dark blot,
To Thee whose blood can cleanse each spot,—
O Lamb of God! I come."

Slips of paper, with that hymn printed on them, had been scattered on the benches. She had taken one with her when she left the room, and had read and re-read it so often, that the night before she could have repeated it all word for word. But this morning her head was in a whirl. Even the few first lines bewildered and confused her; and when at last she had succeeded in recalling two verses, the rest seemed like a medley in her mind, and when she attempted to speak them, passed away from her like a mist. She felt blinded and lost, and put out her hand with a faint, troubled cry. Then there came to her the last words spoken in the old room. She wanted to repeat them, but they floated from her too.

"Dear Father — lead us — with light. —

Dear Father — win us — from sin," she faltered; not in prayer, but in a vain effort to recollect Christy's petitions. But the repetition of the words served to calm her; and when she had so far recalled them as to say connectedly — "Dear Father, lead us with the light of thy blessing," her face grew calm and composed, and her lips ceased their constant restless motion.

For hours she lay there, not sleeping, but in a heavy stupor, — so heavy that she did not waken even when the child upon her arm began to move his hands and limbs with a strange twitching of the muscles which would have agonized the heart of any mother whose loving eyes had watched him; nor even when the tiny form writhed itself out of her grasp in a terrible convulsion. The little figure grew still: the blue eyes stared up through the broken roof, looking perhaps for a Home where it might rest, and for the Elder Brother who had said, "Suffer the little children to come unto me;" and the long-drawn breath labored up painfully through the small chest; but the mother knew nothing of it all.

About three o'clock that afternoon, when the sun was beginning to cast long slant shadows through the trees along the mountain road, Edward Bailey came sauntering up the road, with his hands thrust deep down into his pockets, and his head dropped forward on his breast, as if his whole mind were engaged in studying the stones and earth beneath his feet. If any one had asked him if he were going up the mountain to visit his mother, he would have said "No," in as decided a tone as it was possible for a man to use; nevertheless this was the third time that day that he had found himself (almost in spite of himself) taking the way towards his home. But whatever his first desires and inclinations had been, it was now too late to undertake the journey. Yet he went on in an uncertain, objectless manner, farther and farther, until he had passed quite beyond the turning point of his two earlier walks.

He had paused, to look up at the sun and see how far on in the day it might be, when a sound like a moan of pain struck his ear. He glanced about him, and, seeing no living creature near but a few head of cattle grazing not far away, supposed that some noise which they had made had misled him; and was about to turn back toward the village when the sound came again. There was no mistaking it. It was the groan of some one, — a woman, he thought, — in great distress. The tumble-down barn, which for years had stood as a sort of landmark in the road, was just before him; and he hurried toward it, wondering if some starving tramp had crept in there to die.

There was in this hard, coarse, wicked man one purer vein. Deep down in his heart there lay a little well of sympathy for any thing that was weak or helpless. The waters of that well had been tossing and swelling ever since Frank Austin had spoken to him of the lonely old mother who longed so sorely to see her only child; the sight of the brave young fellow standing up firmly against so many strong and unscrupulous opposers had troubled its waters again; and now the picture which met his eyes, as he stepped into the old barn, touched its very depths.

"Mollie! Why, Mollie Allen! is this you?" he said, hastening to the side of the girl, who, her face flushed with fever, was rolling her head painfully from side to side on the hard floor. "How came you here, Mollie?"

She opened her eyes and looked at him, wildly at first, failing to recognize him, although his face had been familiar to her from her earliest childhood. Then a gleam of intelligence awoke in her eyes, and catching at his hand, she cried eagerly, —

"O Ed! you'll bring him, won't you? You was always good to me, never mind how bad you was to other folks, 'cause I was so lonesome. O Ed, bring him, bring him, quick!"

"Bring who, the doctor? 'Course I will;" and he sprang to his feet, for he had knelt down beside her.

"No! no! Not the doctor. I'm dying, Ed, and no doctor can stop me. I'm dying with my sins all on my head; and there's nobody to help me! I want him. O Ed, go, go!" and she pushed him from her with trembling, burning hands.

"I'll go," he said, soothingly, putting back the hair from her hot face with his big, coarse fingers. "I'll go if you can tell me who you want. Who is it, Mollie?"

"The boy, the Hall boy; him with the holy face," and the great eyes looked beseechingly up into those of the man who bent over her.

"You mean him as was the boss of the meetin' yesterday?"

"Yes, yes. Oh, dear Ed, good Ed! go and fetch him," she cried, imploringly.

"Yes, I'll go. Be quiet, girl; do, or you'll kill yourself. And I'll just stop and fetch the doctor too, for you're awful bad, Mollie."

"Awful bad! Aye, I am awful bad; but it ain't the doctor as can help me. But maybe the boy can. Bring him right away. If you wait to go round by the village, it will be too late. Promise me you'll go straight to the Hall."

She was sitting up now, stretching out her hands in the agony of her entreaty. Bailey laid her back gently, having taken off his coat and folded it for a pillow for her head.

"Lie down," he said, "and I'll be right off. I won't go to the doctor's till I find the other feller and fetch him over. Will you lie still while I'm gone?"

"Yes," she said, more calmly, "only go."

He was leaving her, when his eye fell on the baby lying at some little distance from her. He paused an instant, attracted by the strange, unnatural look on the tiny face.

"He's fast asleep, poor little man," said Mary, feebly. "Lay him close to me."

He lifted the child, bending his ear cautiously to its lips, to see if it were breathing, — for the waxen face looked more like death than life, — but he could hear the workings of its laboring chest, and its little limbs hung limp, not stiff and cold; and so he laid it down beside the mother, saying nothing, but wondering in his mind, as he went away, whether either woman or child would be living when he returned.

"Austin," said Charlie Grant, running up to Frank, as he stood on the play-ground, bat in hand, arranging some of the preliminaries of a game of base ball, "there's a man here that want's to see you. Ed Bailey, he says his name is."

"Oh, yes," said Austin, "I know;" and the color rose in his face somewhat.

"I knew him, too, as soon as I saw him. He's that fellow that made the boys sit down and behave themselves, when they were making such a noise yesterday. I wonder if he's come to apologize for them?"

"Not much, I guess, Charlie," replied Austin, laughing. "Here, Tom, I'm wanted; take my place, will you?" and he tossed his bat to Tom Morrison, who stood near him. "Go on without me."

Bailey was waiting at some distance from the players; and as Frank walked rapidly toward him, wondering what his errand might be, he came quickly forward to meet him.

"Can you go along of me, right off?" he said abruptly, as soon as Austin was within hearing. "There's a woman very sick down here, and she wants yer."

"You have made some mistake," said Austin, looking much perplexed. "It cannot be me you want."

"Yes, it is, too," replied the man, roughly. "She said as 'twas the one what was boss of that 'ere meetin' down to the Widder Tracy's.

Come on, now," he added, anxiously. "If you wait to stand fussin' about it, she'll die afore you get there. She's awful sick. I know it's you she wants for she said so," he went on, seeing that Frank still looked very doubtful. "She was at the meetin' yesterday, and she seen you there. Maybe you seen her there; she had a bit of a baby with her."

"Oh, yes," said Frank, "I remember her. I noticed she looked very badly yesterday."

"She's been kind of ailin' this long while back, but she must have been took pretty sudden at the last. But come along, I'll tell you as we go on; there ain't no time to lose, I'm afeared."

"One moment, Bailey," said Austin, anxiously. "I am more than ready to do any thing for the poor woman; but I'm nothing but a boy. If she is so ill, she ought to have a doctor and a minister, not a young fellow like me. I wouldn't know what to do for her."

"Yes, you would too," replied Bailey, speaking even more roughly than usual in his intense eagerness. "It's just a boy she wants. She called you 'boy,' all the while she was a screechin' and beggin' for you. Come, come! I tell you, you shall come!" and he advanced a step nearer and grasped Frank's arm angrily, as he saw that he still hesitated.

"Why, Austin, what is all this about?"

Never had Frank been more glad to hear Dr. Drayton's voice. His perplexity and bewilderment were set at rest almost immediately; for no sooner had the Doctor heard the story than, at once comprehending the situation, he advised him by all means to go with Bailey.

"Mrs. Morton can go with you with such things as the woman needs," he said, "and I will drive to the parsonage and let Mr. Leonard know the state of affairs. I was going down to Graydon this afternoon, at any rate. Perhaps Dr. Buford could drive over to the barn, if I stop there and tell him of this sad case. I will go to the house at once, and let Mrs. Morton prepare whatever is necessary. She will not detain you more than fifteen minutes."

"Fifteen minutes!" said Bailey, harshly. "Do you suppose that woman will care what you bring her, if she's got to pay for it by waitin' fifteen minutes? Didn't you hear me tell yer she was dyin'; and do yer think Death's a goin' to stand waitin' for fifteen minutes, while you stuff a basket with goodies as she's too far gone to touch? Come, boy," and he turned from the Doctor to Austin, "if you've got a spark of that mercy you was a talkin' about yesterday, come to the poor creetur, for I bet she's screamin' for yer like mad long afore this."

"Go, Austin," said the doctor, as Frank looked at him for an answer to this appeal. "Mrs. Morton and I will follow you as soon as practicable."

The words had scarcely left his lips when

Bailey, catching Austin by the sleeve, hurried him away; and in another moment the two were out of sight. On their way to Mary's place of shelter, Bailey told Frank all he knew; but that was but little, except so far as the girl's every-day life was concerned; and it was with the sensation of accepting and undertaking a work for which he was totally unprepared and incompetent, and to which he was entirely new, that the boy entered the dilapidated old barn.

They had heard her voice talking wildly and despairingly as they neared the spot, and when they entered, she lay with her face covered with her hands. She did not remove her hands, nor notice them in any way, until Bailey, going close to her, said, in a tone more gentle than Frank had supposed him capable of using, —

"Mollie, here's the chap you wanted to see."

She opened her eyes and looked at him;

then stretched out both her hands, crying imploringly, —

"Come and tell me! Oh, come and tell me! The old man said God would take us back; but you keep saying 'Just as I am — just as I am!' You ring it in my ears all the while, and I can't go back just as I am. I've sinned and sinned, more than such as you know; and how can I go just as I am? Tell me. You're brave and good. I saw it in your face yesterday, and I see it now, though you look so pitiful at me. I'm dying, boy; remember that, and tell me what I'm to do. Oh, hear how they sing it over and over again — 'Just as I am'" —

> "'poor, wretched, blind,
> Sight, riches, healing of the mind,
> Yea, all I need in Thee to find, —
> O Lamb of God! I come.'"

She ceased her tossing to and fro, and the fierce pushing aside of the imaginary enemies who seemed to be repeating the refrain for her torment, to look into Frank's face, as his calm, steady voice spoke the sweet words clearly and distinctly: —

>"'Just as I am, — thou wilt receive,
> Wilt pardon, comfort, cleanse, relieve;
> Because thy promise I believe, —
> O Lamb of God! I come.'"

Her face was growing less and less wild. She lay looking up at him for a few moments without speaking; then she said feebly, —

"Sins, sins as black as night. My soul is covered with them."

"Yes, I know," said Frank, gently; "but if you are sorry for them Jesus will wash them all away. Ask Him to make your soul white and pure. Go to Him now, and ask Him. This very moment. You need not even move; ask Him as you lie here."

"Just as I am?" she asked, finding the words suited to her need, and Frank answered, —

> "'Just as I am, — and waiting not
> To rid my soul of one dark blot, —
> To Thee whose blood can cleanse each spot,
> O Lamb of God! I come.'"

Again she lay and looked at him, at first with a little brightness in her face; but soon it clouded again, her lips trembled and quivered, and she said with a despairing sob in her voice, —

"I would, I want to; but I'm afraid."

"I dare say you are afraid," said Frank, tenderly, taking one of the hot hands, and stroking it with his cool fingers. "Jesus' love is so great that we cannot understand it, and are almost afraid at first to believe in it. But it is all true. He died to save us. He died that He might wash us in His blood and cleanse us from our sins. There are two verses more in our hymn. Let us say them to Jesus like a little prayer: —

> "'Just as I am, — though tossed about
> With many a conflict, many a doubt,
> Fightings within and fears without, —
> O Lamb of God! I come.

"'Just as I am, — Thy love unknown
Has broken every barrier down,
Now to be Thine, yea, Thine alone, —
O Lamb of God! I come.'"

Her eyes were closed when the last words left his lips; and, thinking that she might be sinking into a doze, he did not move. Some one, — Bailey, he supposed, — made a slight noise at the door-way, and he raised his hand to silence him; but did not turn for fear that he might disturb her. After a while she stirred a little, her lips moved, and bending his head he heard the one word, "Wonderful!" whispered as if to herself. Just then Dr. Buford came softly in, looked at her, and went out. She moved again.

"Where's baby?" she asked, quietly.

Glancing downward, she saw the little face resting against her arm. She watched it for a moment, then she looked at Frank.

"Did you know?" she whispered.

He did not answer at once, for he was uncertain whether her mind was wandering or not.

"He has gone before his mother," she said quietly, without even a tremor in her voice. "Dear little baby. Mother's little blessing."

The dark lashes fell again on the sunken cheeks. Dr. Buford stole in, hearing her voice, and Frank motioned him toward the baby. He leaned down and looked into the small face, shook his head, and as the mother stirred, moved back out of sight. It might trouble her to see him, and his skill was useless here.

But she did not open her eyes. Her baby's face was the last she saw on earth; for when, an hour after, the blue-veined lids were slowly raised, the dark eyes were looking up toward the sky which shone down upon her through the broken roofing. A moment she lay gazing upward, a bright smile playing softly on her lips, her hand still clasping Austin's fingers.

"Just as I am — Love unknown — Thine alone."

The sweet smile faded, the hand loosened its clasp; and Frank rose very quietly, and went out to the little group in the doorway.

VII.

JOE MILWARD'S VISIT.

FOR a week or two it seemed as if the prayer-meeting in Mrs. Tracy's room were likely to prove a great success. The school-boys were interested in it; partly because it was something new, and partly because they had all been much touched by the story of Mary Allen. With the people at the Corner the interest was very much of the same order; and for three or four Sabbaths the room was so well filled, that Frank was delighted with the result of his effort.

But little by little the number decreased. The boys began to tire of it. After all, it was very like other prayer-meetings; and the morning and evening services in the church were about enough, they thought, without a third meeting in the afternoon. Will Seaton persevered for about a month in his attendance, and then came to Frank one afternoon with the announcement that he didn't feel very "full of sing," and he guessed he wouldn't go down to Milward's that day.

That defection was one of some importance, for there was not a voice in the school to equal Will's; but Frank made no objection, and managed as best he could with regard to a chorister, asking assistance from one and another from Sabbath to Sabbath, for Will did not volunteer his services again. The little company dwindled and dwindled, until at last there were at times none present except Frank, Laurence Bronson, Christy and his boys, and the old woman who had come in on that first Sabbath, and had been a regular attendant ever since.

Edward Bailey had never made his appearance there since Mary Allen's death. Frank had hoped much from the feeling he had manifested for her; but apparently his hopes were groundless, for the report of his misdoings rather grew than lessened, and he avoided all intercourse with Austin with studied pertinacity. More than once Frank had attempted on meeting him to draw him into conversation; but all his efforts were repelled with contemptuous indifference. Perhaps, if the boy had known that Bailey invariably took up his position on Sabbath afternoons outside the tavern, where he could hear every word of the hymns as they floated out through the open windows, and could often catch whole sentences of the short addresses and the Scripture which was read, he would have felt less disheartened with regard to him. Somehow he had taken a special interest in this young man. He was not a little disappointed when he found him so utterly unapproachable; and there was so little to encourage him that the disappointment affected

JOE MILWARD'S VISIT. 145

him more seriously than it might otherwise have done.

"You're not losing heart, are you, Frank?" asked Laurence, as they walked down toward the Corner one beautiful afternoon.

Frank had scarcely spoken since they left the Hall; and was tramping silently along the road, with a face whose gravity betokened very serious thought.

"No, scarcely that," he answered. "Things don't look very hopeful just now, we must confess; but they must look a good deal worse than this before I give up the ship. I was thinking, when you spoke, what a grand help Allan Haywood would have been if he had been with us. Dear old boy! He was such a quiet fellow and yet such a regular go-ahead in any thing like this."

"Yes, and it isn't only in this sort of thing that we miss him," replied Laurence, gravely. "The Hall misses him, Frank. He gave our set a tone which made it felt all through the school. We are not what we used to be when Allan Haywood influenced — with his will or against it — every boy in our class. That fellow's high standard of right and wrong, and steadfast adherence to that standard, did more for us than he knew, or than we knew, either."

They walked on in silence for some time, thinking of the boy of whom they had been speaking. He had been the close friend of both six months ago; but he was called Home to his Father's House above, when, as it seemed, his work on earth was but just begun.

There was a tender feeling pervading the whole school with regard to Allan, for he had been, very shortly before his death, the victim of a cruel fraud which had brought him under deep disgrace; and it was only a few days before he was taken away, that the author of the mischief, Arthur Bentley, was discovered, and Allan reinstated in the love and confidence of his teachers and school-mates. It was this which had made Arthur such a Pariah in the Hall. Neither he nor his brother, Professor Bentley, had ever been favorites among the boys; but since the day on which Arthur's crime had been made known, his companions, in their utter contempt for his sin, and fierce anger at having been deceived by him to the injury of Haywood, had almost ignored his existence among them. Will Seaton, once his best friend, had never spoken to him since the occurrence; and the boy walked among his fellows as entirely alone, perhaps more so, than if he had been upon a desert island in the midst of an unknown sea. Mr. Grau's efforts, on the day of the picnic, and the aid he had given Tom Morrison in saving Miss Churchill from her great peril on the same day, had done something towards giving him a less trying position in the school; but even now the place he held was far from being an enviable post.

When the boys entered their room that afternoon, they saw at once that affairs had taken a new turn either for the better or the worse. At the first glance, they noticed among the unusually large number collected within the old walls an air of expectancy and interest; and, looking round to discover if possible the cause of the suppressed excitement, Austin saw, seated in a corner, a wiry little man, between whom and himself the attention of the company seemed to be divided. He knew the man at once; he was Joe Milward, the proprietor of the tavern next door. What was he here for? Certainly for no good, if one were to judge from the expression of his small eyes, and thick, heavy lips.

The truth was, that Milward had determined by some means or other to put a stop to these meetings. If Frank were dismayed by Bailey's conduct, he was no less so. For the past two weeks, Edward had absented himself very frequently from the evening carousals at the tavern, and on this Sabbath and the preceding one had not entered its doors at all. Going out to seek him, Milward had found him on the afternoon of each Sabbath beneath the windows of Mrs. Tracy's room; and although a knot of young fellows were standing around him, making all manner of fun of the services going on above them, the tavern-keeper was sharp enough to see that Bailey joined with but little spirit in the mockery.

Besides this, he had refused more than once on some frivolous pretext, within the last few days, to lend his aid in the petty robberies of hen-roosts and the like, by which the loungers about Milward's were in the habit of supplying their wants; and all these "notions," as he termed them, of Bailey's were ascribed by the wily tavern-keeper to Austin's influence. To be sure, Edward laughed at the efforts of the Hall boys quite as sneeringly as any of his companions; but that did not blind Milward to the fact that the young man had been restless and uneasy in his mind ever since the day of the first meeting. He could not well afford to lose Bailey's influence, nor his presence from his bar-room; and he had fully determined to make an end of these troublesome gatherings in Mrs. Tracy's room, if opposition and threats could accomplish his purpose.

Looking at him as he sat in his corner, his dark face sharply outlined against the white-washed wall, Frank felt sure that he had come with some evil intention, and fully expected that the meeting would be rudely interrupted, perhaps noisily broken up. But he was mistaken. The services went on as usual, disturbed from time to time by laughing and talking among the boys, but entirely unmolested by Milward and the three or four coarse-looking men who sat near him. The tavern-keeper wanted to know what it was that had spoiled Edward Bailey's thorough enjoyment of wickedness for wickedness' sake, and so he sat quietly attentive until the meeting was drawing to its close. Then he rose, in the moment's pause between the last hymn and the dismission of the little company by Christy, and, turning towards Austin, said in a manner as impertinent as contemptuous tone, sneering lip, and defiant brow could make it, —

"You said, young man, a while back, that this meetin,' or whatever you call it, was open for any remarks. I've got one remark to make. If you know when you're well off you'll attend to that, and then I'll have no more to say; but if you don't take heed to it, you'll hear a few words more from Joe Milward that you may like still less. My remark is just this: You've got to put a stop to all this cant and fuss. I won't put up with it."

If Frank Austin's natural pride and haughtiness had not been already brought under strong control, he must then and there have forfeited what little influence he had gained in his unfruitful field by a sudden outburst of angry retort; for the man's insulting look, words, and manner, were insufferable. Even calm, composed old Christy turned sharply toward him, his wrinkled face flushing and trembling with indignant feeling.

But the very manner of his being led into the kingdom of his Lord had struck a heavy blow at Austin's self-reliance and self-esteem, and for months past he had been fighting with this proud spirit; and, though often worsted for the time, had gained upon it slowly but surely. Not one word of anger passed his firmly set lips, as he stood for a moment looking at Milward. When at length he did speak, it was in a constrained, unnatural voice, and his words were very few.

"You must allow me my right," he said, "to worship God as I see fit under my own roof. The meeting will now be dismissed."

His calmness infuriated Milward; but he

saw plainly enough that it was forced; and hoping to destroy it, and thereby create a disturbance which would for ever end all Austin's efforts in the neighborhood, he motioned Christy, who had already stepped forward, to one side, and speaking, if possible, more insolently than before, said, —

"Your right! I'd like to know who has any rights at this corner but Joe Milward! Ain't it been called 'Milward's Corner' these five years? Now look-a-here, youngster! you may stand up there, and defy me with that proud face of yourn all day; but I tell you if you show it here next Sunday you'll get it washed in mud, and then ducked in yonder mill-pond, so sure as my name's Joe Milward. That's the other remark I spoke of. Now look out for yourself!" and, with a snap of his fingers almost in Frank's face, the man walked out of the room.

He had seen that he could not urge him to a quarrel, and keen enough to know that in a war of words he would be worsted before his own allies, he left the field. He was instantly followed by his friends, and Frank and Laurence, with Christy, were left in undisturbed possession, for the present at least.

"Will he do what he says, Christy?" asked Laurence, anxiously, as Frank, turning his face from them, stood looking out of the window.

"He will, sir, unless force is used to prevent him. I think, sir, that we've done all we can here. One soul has been brought into light and joy through these little gatherin's. Let us thank the Lord for that. He may open the way for us some time to bring the blessin' of His Gospel to more. But, Mr. Austin, dear lad," and he laid his hand tenderly on Frank's shoulder, "I'm thinkin' He isn't ready just yet. It has been dangersome from the first; and now we'll need to give it up, and just wait a bit. Milward will keep his word, but so keep it as the law can't touch him, he's that cute and knowin'. He's a terrible, dangerous man, sir, is Milward. It's really not safe for you to try it again. I thanked the Lord — indeed, I thanked Him hearty — when I saw Joe safe out of the room this afternoon, and you unhurt, Mr. Frank."

"I thanked Him, too," said Austin, turning toward him with a smile.

"And you will run no risks, sir?" pleaded the old man. "Or at least you will tell the Doctor all about this?" he added, feeling very sure that Dr. Drayton would keep the boy from venturing too far in his enthusiasm.

"Certainly, I shall. He always asks me the result of each service here, and he shall know every thing. I think with you, Christy, that we'll need to pause and consider a little; but I don't believe that God is closing this door against us. We had better go down now, and consult as to our future plans at some other time."

No one spoke to or molested them as they

left the house, although there was quite a company gathered on the piazza of the tavern, who watched them curiously as they walked up the road.

VIII.

A FLASH OF THE DIAMOND.

DR. DRAYTON had listened very gravely to the account of the events of the afternoon; and when it was concluded, he sat for some moments without speaking, drumming with one hand upon the table beside which he happened to be sitting, with a look on his face which Austin felt boded no good to the continuance of his enterprise.

"This is rather a serious business," he said, at length.

"Yes, sir," replied Frank, eagerly, "it does look a little serious; but you don't think that we'll have to give it up, do you? I don't feel as if I possibly could."

The doctor smiled that little, grave half-smile of his that Frank had learned to love, as he said : —

"It will be a great disappointment to you, I know, Austin; but I am afraid that it will have to be so. I would confide in Christopher Dunn's judgment far more than in my own, as regards the feeling and the probable action of these people; and according to your own testimony it is his opinion that Milward will execute his threats. No one would be more glad than I to see a reformation effected in that lawless place, but your father would never pardon me if any evil should befall you there."

Yes, — Austin knew that, perhaps even better than Dr. Drayton. His father, a bitter scoffer at all that was holy and good, had so far, since his son had avowed himself a soldier in Christ's army, contented himself with light jestings and banter on the subject, thinking this new idea a mere boyish fancy, out of which he might with ease be ridiculed. But the boy knew that he would look upon his new purpose in life with very different eyes if it brought him into any difficulty or danger, and would hold Dr. Drayton sharply responsible if any trouble arose at the Corner. He had not concealed his plan from his parents, but Mr. and Mrs. Austin knew little of " Milward's," save that it was a poorly kept and shabby tavern; and when Frank had written that he intended to establish a Sabbath-afternoon service there, the announcement had been received by his father with shouts of laughter, and by his mother with a protest against his association with such a class of people.

" He will be sure to catch some horrid fever, or something of that sort," she had exclaimed, when her husband, telling her that he had a grand joke for her, read the letter aloud.

" Not at all," said Mr. Austin; " there is no danger of that. For my part, I am delighted. Like all young converts, as they call them, he is running the thing into the ground, and he'll sicken of the whole business in a month's time."

The mocking letter he had received in reply had shown Frank that his intention, as it then stood, was a matter of perfect indifference, or at the most only one of amusement, to his father; but he knew very well that if Mr. Austin suspected the present state of affairs, he would at once forbid the further continuance of the meetings, and would moreover severely blame Dr. Drayton if he permitted his son to carry them on.

"I am sorry," said the Doctor, as the boy sat, with drooping head, and anxious, discouraged face before him, attempting no answer to his last remark. "I am more sorry than I can tell you that this mission has failed so soon. And yet, Austin, you have realized a rich reward. That poor girl's tossed and troubled soul might have been lost in the dark waters, if it had not been for those little gatherings. You told me, my son," and he laid his hand kindly on Austin's bowed head, "when you first thought of establishing these meetings, that you were 'just hungry' to do something for Christ. Your Master knew the longing, the hunger of your soul; and I think that He has fed you with the finest of the wheat. It seems as if He were for the present taking the work out of your hands; let Him see that while you are ready, and more than ready, to give your strength to Him, you are also prepared, if it be His will, to *wait* on the Lord. Now it is time for us to go down to church. I heard the procession filing through the hall a few moments since, and I presume they are waiting for us."

They left the room together, Frank taking his place among the boys in the lower hall, as they fell into line ready to march down to the Graydon Church; and the Doctor saw no more of him until, happening to turn his head during the sermon, he caught a glimpse of the boy's face as he sat in the pew adjoining his own.

Evidently he was thinking but little of the sermon, if one were to judge from his anxious, troubled expression. From the bottom of his heart, Dr. Drayton pitied him; for he knew well with what an enthusiasm of devotion, and of enjoyment too, the boy had undertaken his work, the whole fabric of which now seemed to be lying in ruin at his feet. He felt sorry that he had been forced to dissuade him from persevering in it; sorry also that their interview had closed so abruptly and unsatisfactorily. The longer he watched his flurried, flushed face, the more he wanted to do something to console and cheer him.

The service was concluded, and Frank was turning to leave the seat, when Mrs. Drayton, who sat at the head of the master's pew, touched his arm and whispered, —

"The Doctor wants you to wait for him at the gate."

"I have to see Dr. Buford to-night," said Dr. Drayton, as he reached the entrance to the church-grounds, where Frank was waiting for him, "and I thought that we might walk down there together, and finish the conversation which the church-bell interrupted. You look as if the air might rest and invigorate you."

"I should like it very much, sir," said Frank, gratefully.

Turning away from the gate, they walked slowly down to the road towards Dr. Buford's house, which stood on the outskirts of the village, talking earnestly as they went; the boy, in his ardor and enthusiasm, using every argument he could employ to urge his plea; the man, kindly, but resistlessly, putting them all down one by one; trying to throw in little crumbs of comfort and encouragement by the way, but steadily discountenancing the pursuance of his desire. Poor Frank! He was in no mood, when they reached the end of their journey, to go in and sit down for a long conversation with chatty Mrs. Buford. He opened the gate for Dr. Drayton, but did not pass through himself.

"Would there be any objection to my waiting for you out here, sir?" he asked, as the Doctor looked inquiringly at him. "I had rather not go in."

"Certainly not. Meet me at the cross-road below at half-past nine. It is now nine," he added, as he pulled out his watch and held it toward Frank, in order that he might compare it with his own.

"I will be on hand, sir;" and the boy strolled away toward a piece of woods which lay on the opposite side of the road.

The moon was shining brightly, and the woods were almost as light as if it were day. It looked calm and peaceful and quiet beneath the trees, and Frank turned in among their leafy branches with the hope that his own restlessness and anxiety would be calmed by a walk through the cool, soft shadows.

But scarcely had he stepped off the main road when he was suddenly seized from behind, while two rough, coarse hands crossed his face, one blinding his eyes, the other closing his mouth. For an instant he struggled to free himself; but the next he was borne heavily down to the ground, with those hard hands still pressing close upon his lips and eyes.

Evidently there were at least three in the party which had attacked him; powerful fellows too, if he judged from their handling. He was not hurt, and he lay quite still trying to think what was best for him to do, whether to lie quiet, or to attempt to throw them from him and make his escape; wondering too how it was that they had stolen upon him so unobserved, for they had come from the road, not from the wood-land. Then he remembered that as he had stood with Dr. Drayton at the gate of Dr. Buford's place, five men had passed them, rough-looking fellows, bound, as he had supposed, for the tavern at the other extremity of the village. If he had recollected that they were so near, he might not have thought it safe to leave the road; but he had quite forgotten the fact of their having passed him; and besides, the woods were not thick, but light, well cleared of under-brush, and used constantly as a road from Graydon to Milton, — a little settlement four miles farther up the turnpike.

While Frank and the Doctor were talking earnestly of the occurrences of the afternoon in the library at Drayton Hall, the affair had been discussed with no less animation in the bar-room of the tavern. The result of his attack upon the young leader of the new enterprise had been a great disappointment to Joseph Milward; and the more he thought of it, the more plainly he saw that he had been worsted in the encounter, and the hotter grew his wrath against this interference with his so-called " rights." Besides all this, Edward Bailey was again absent from the bar, and had led away with him two or three of Milward's most constant customers. Altogether the list of Austin's offences was growing longer and longer every moment. No words were too fierce and rough to be applied to him, no curses too deep to be muttered against him, until finally the man had worked himself up to a perfect fury of hatred and anger against the " usurper," as he chose to call him.

His abuse and invectives had excited the half-tipsy crowd of men and boys who filled the room to almost as great a pitch of passion as that to which he had brought himself; and when he declared that Edward Bailey was fast going over to the enemy, and that in a short time, he, the quickest-witted and most successful rogue among them, would be lost to them, the room fairly rang again with loud threats and denunciations. Angry declarations that the thing should be stopped at once; that they would not even wait until the next Sabbath, to see whether the interlopers had been daunted by the experience of that afternoon; that the first time they caught the instigator of all this mischief, they would duck him in the mill-pond as Milward had threatened, and so forth, filled the air; until the host, satisfied that the work would be done without his personal aid, began to choose his words with a little more care, lest, if serious evil came to his rivals, he should be held responsible.

After a time the tumult had somewhat subsided; and William Simpson, the man who at the first meeting in Mrs. Tracy's room had so violently opposed the offering of prayer, had, together with three or four younger men, strolled down the village street for a little walk; intending, however, to return to the tavern to spend the hours of the night in their customary manner.

The little party, all half-intoxicated, had passed Dr. Buford's house just as Frank declined going in with the Doctor; and no sooner had they parted, than Simpson, whose dislike to Austin was almost as bitter as that which Milward entertained towards him, proposed to his companions that they should then and there execute their purpose, and so prevent at once all further annoyance from him. The plan was instantly agreed to, half in earnest, half in joke; and Simpson had led them into the woods before they had time to repent of their decision. The capture had been made easily enough, the boy being totally unsuspecting and unprepared; and Simpson hurried them on, anxious lest they should be discovered before their purpose was accomplished.

"Bring him along to the pond," he said roughly, as the others having aided him in throwing Frank to the ground, stood laughing heartily at the success of their plan. "If you don't look out he'll give us the slip, or some one will come by, and we'll have to run for it. Lend a hand here, and lift him up. We'll cut through the woods to the old mill. There'll be nobody there to meddle with us, and if he don't get such a sousin' as 'll wash the stiffness out of him, it won't be my fault."

It was of no use to struggle. Simpson's hands were across his face, his heavy knee pressing, not painfully, but still resistlessly, upon his chest. After the first effort to spring up, which had been met by the instant seizure of four pairs of strong hands, and a muttered, "If you don't want to be hurt, youngster, you'd best lie still," Frank submitted to the force of circumstances, his blood boiling at the insult, but his judgment convincing him that opposition was worse than useless. In another moment he was raised from the ground, and with smothered laughter and coarse jests, borne rapidly through the woods.

The journey was not a long one. The pond, a stagnant, muddy piece of water, lying under the shadow of a long-disused mill, almost touched the borders of the wood a quarter of a mile away on the opposite side, and his bearers were not long in reaching it.

"Now for it," exclaimed Simpson. "I'll keep his eyes covered. Pitch him clear into the middle, and then run for it before he rises."

"Wait a bit," said one of the group, his heart failing him at the last moment. "Give him one chance. Maybe he'll engage never to come nigh us again, if we let him off this time. Will you, Snobby, on yer honor, promise never to hold no more o' them meetin's? If not, here you go. Will you promise?"

Simpson lifted his hand from the boy's lips, and the answer he had expected came firm and clear, —

"No, never!"

"In with him, then. One, two, three! Over he goes!"

"Not if my name's Ed Bailey!"

The whole party stumbled and staggered

backward, almost dropping their burden; for two powerful hands caught the helpless figure as they swung it forward, seizing it with such strength that the sudden recoil almost brought them all to the ground.

Startled and confounded, the men slightly loosened their grasp. Frank made a spring, but they were too quick for him. Their hold upon him tightened again; and, with an oath, Simpson exclaimed, —

"Stand away, Bailey! It's none of your business."

"It is my business, too. Put him down, you mean scamps, fightin' five to one. I wouldn't give an old shoe to buy the hull crowd of yer. Put him down, I say."

"Hold on to him, boys," said Simpson, seeing that his allies looked rather hesitating; "we'll duck him yet. He's got this feller right under his thumb, you see. Now for it!"

Frank felt himself swung forward again. He struggled furiously to free himself; Bailey's hands still held him fast, and between the two, the attempt was for the second time defeated.

Austin heard a low, muttered curse; a scuffle, — a heavy fall. Then he was suddenly lifted into the air, flung forward, and the next instant he felt the green, slimy waters of the pond close above his head.

In another moment he had risen to the surface, and was striking out for the shore. To his surprise, no opposition was offered to his landing; and, scrambling up to the bank, he sat down to wipe from his face the drops of thick, muddy water which blinded his eyes.

It was very still, and turning around to look about him as soon as his eyes were sufficiently cleared to see, he found that he was alone. At least he thought himself so on the first glance; but rising to his feet, he saw a motionless figure stretched upon the grass. It was but the work of a moment to spring forward, bend over the prostrate form, and lift the heavy head from the sharp stone upon which it lay.

"Bailey! Ed!" whispered the boy, striving to stanch with his water-soaked handkerchief the stream of blood which was flowing from a deep cut on the man's head. "Can you speak?"

There was no answer: the head lay like a lump of lead upon his knees; and the great, powerful hands hung limp and helpless when he lifted them. For a moment Frank sat watching him; then he tied his handkerchief tightly around the wounded head, and laying it gently down upon the grass, ran swiftly back through the road over which he had just been carried, toward the village; and a loud, sharp peal at the door-bell soon called Dr. Buford to his assistance.

IX.

HIDDEN MANNA.

"WHY, Frank Austin!" cried the astonished doctor, as the drenched, pale figure in the doorway met his sight. "What has happened to you?"

"Jump into the carriage, quick!" gasped Frank, having seen to his great joy, as he rushed up the private road, that the doctor's carriage was just turning from the house to the stable. "He's hurt. I'm afraid he's dying."

"Who? Dr. Drayton?" and the physician whistled with a sharp, peculiar intonation which his coachman understood, as he snatched his hat from the rack, and hurried out upon the piazza.

"What is it, Frank? There's the carriage. Jump in, and tell me as we go."

"No, no, not there; the other way!" and Frank grasped the reins as Dr. Buford turned his horse's head toward Drayton Hall. "Drive toward Milton. It's Edward Bailey; he is almost killed."

"But what is this all about?" asked the physician, as his horse trotted rapidly down the road. "I thought that you were to meet Dr. Drayton two hours ago at the cross-roads. He certainly told me so. And yet here you are, drenched to the skin, come for help for this Bailey. I am completely befogged, boy. What does it all mean?"

"I hardly know myself," replied Frank. "But I had scarcely more than parted from Dr. Drayton at your door, when I was seized by a party of those roughs from around Milward's, and carried off to the old mill-pond, to be ducked, it seems. The rascals had me, for there were five of them, — big fellows, too, they must have been; and there's no knowing what might have been the end of it if it hadn't been for Bailey. He dashed in on the scene very unexpectedly, so far as I could gather, just as they had lifted me up to throw me, and caught me back. They had covered my eyes so that I should not identify them, I suppose, so I cannot tell exactly what went on; but I heard a violent quarrel between them, then the sound of a scuffle and a fall, and I was pitched overboard in less time than it takes to tell it. I wasn't hurt, though; and as soon as I could make my way out of the mess with which I was covered, I scrambled up the bank, to find to my astonishment and dismay that there was at least one fellow who had not escaped so easily. Poor Bailey must have been thrown in the fight, and have struck full upon the edge of that sharp ledge of rock which crops out above the pond. You remember it, I suppose, sir?"

"Yes. Is he badly cut?"

"Very badly, I'm afraid. He was senseless when I left him."

So he was still, when they reached him. He lay just as Frank had placed him, his face turned up toward the sky, his hands stretched out on either side, helpless and still.

"Who did this?" asked the doctor, as he bent over him.

"I don't know, sir. The voice fiercest in the quarrel sounded like that of a man who was very violent at one of our little meetings when they were first started; but they kept my eyes covered, as I said, and when I reached the bank again after they had thrown me into the water, there was not a living soul here but this poor fellow. They must have run when they saw what they had done. He is not dead, is he, doctor?" and Frank bent anxiously over his would-be protector, with a feeling almost of love swelling up in his heart.

"No, not dead, but as near it as a man

need to be. His head is frightfully injured. I have some ugly work to do here. Have you nerve enough to help me? It ought to be done before he is moved; and the night is so bright that I shall have no difficulty, if you can give me a little assistance."

"I can do all you wish, I think, sir," replied Austin.

"Ugly work" it was to watch, as the sharp instruments did their cruel-looking duty; but Frank stood it very well, and felt richly repaid when, having bound up the man's head, and washed the blood from his face, the doctor said in a tone of great satisfaction:

"There, the worst is over and he has not felt it. He might have died on the road if we had not been able to stanch that stream. You have done something towards repaying him, Austin."

Lifting Bailey into the carriage, they drove slowly toward the village. The movement seemed to rouse him a little. He opened his eyes after a moment, tried to lift his hand, and muttered thickly, —

" No, no. Five against one."

Then the heavy eyelids closed again, and he lay quiet until they reached Graydon.

" Where can we take him ? " had been Frank's question when Bailey had been placed in the carriage; and the doctor had told him of a woman who owned a cottage near his own house, who, he thought, would be glad to take care of the man for a slight remuneration until such time as his mother could reach him, and would board both mother and son if that arrangement proved desirable.

Passing his own home, Dr. Buford turned up a cross-road, and stopped at the door of a trim-looking little house, standing in the midst of a pretty garden. It was now past midnight; but in answer to the physician's loud rap on the door, a head was thrust out of the window, and a somewhat startled voice asked, —

"Who's there?"

"Dr. Buford, Mrs. Marsh. Can you take in a poor fellow who has been hurt."

"Yes, sir;" and the head disappeared from the window, to reappear after a very short interval at the open door.

It was no easy matter to lift that heavy, helpless figure into the house, and the doctor no less than Frank was glad that Mrs. Marsh's spare-room opened from the hall, almost touching the front door.

"We'll put him here, poor fellow," said the kind-hearted woman, "because it's bright and sunny of a morning; and I doubt, doctor," with a glance at Bailey as he lay motionless on the bed where they had placed him, "I doubt he'll not leave it this many a day."

"No; it will be a long and hard pull for him, if he gets through at all," said the doctor. "Now let us have him undressed and comfortably in bed. He will probably wake in delirium, and he may rouse up at any moment."

Austin would-fain have remained to assist as far as possible, but the doctor would not allow it. Reminding him that Dr. Drayton must be almost frantic with anxiety on his account, he advised him to go at once to the Hall, only pausing to leave word at his own house that he had brought the wounded man to Mrs. Marsh, and that he wanted his coachman to come to him there immediately.

The fact was that Dr. Buford looked forward to a night of horror with poor Bailey. Fully aware of his habits, he saw that there was every reason to expect a delirium of the wildest kind when he awoke from the stupor in which he now lay; and he knew that Frank had had quite excitement enough for one evening. So, much against his will, Austin left the house to go up to the Hall.

At the physician's gate he met Dr. Drayton, just starting for the old mill. He had stopped as by appointment at the cross-roads; and at half-past nine, Frank not having appeared to keep his part of the engagement, had gone on with his usual unswerving adherence to his purpose, supposing that Austin would overtake him. But when he had reached the Hall, and had waited half an hour in his study, he grew very uneasy, and started out again, expecting to meet him on the road. Reaching Dr. Buford's house, his anxiety increasing every moment, he went in, in the hope that Austin, misunderstanding him, might have stopped there; and, finding him gone, lingered longer than he was aware of in the physician's pleasant parlor. It was a forlorn hope, for it was now very late in the evening, but it was the only one he could find to cling to. There, to his great relief, he found Mrs. Buford, who told him as much as she had been able to gather from Frank's incoherent story; and when the boy met him at the gate, he was on his way to the mill, to see if he could render them any aid. Thankful enough he was to see him unhurt, especially when he had heard the story Frank had to tell; and when he bade him " Good night," having given his consent to Mrs. Buford's plea that he might remain with her until the morning, the common, every-day words were spoken with such earnestness, that Frank felt that they meant more than they had ever meant to him before.

"Good night, sir," he said, and wrung the doctor's hand with a force, which showed that he had appreciated the strong feeling which betrayed itself in the utterance of those two little words.

Dr. Buford's fears with regard to Bailey proved only too true. He lay for an hour or two after Frank had left the house in the stupor in which the boy had seen him; then he roused, first with incoherent murmurs, which grew louder and more intelligible, until at last his frenzy became so fierce and wild, that it required the united strength of his three attendants to restrain him from springing from the bed. His shouts and cries were terrible to hear; and his strength so great, that when morning dawned Dr. Buford had to send for assistance, it being impossible for himself and his man to control him.

For three weeks he lay in that pleasant, sunny room in Mrs. Marsh's cottage, raving in delirium, or lying for hours breathing heavily, with half-closed eyes which noticed nothing that passed around him. Gentle hands ministered to all his needs; a mother's loving eyes dropped tears of pity on the forehead drawn and wrinkled with pain; low voices whispered at the door kind inquiries for him; merry, boyish faces grew grave and tender as the oft-repeated answer came back, "The doctor thinks he cannot live;" and the usually noisy, trampling feet crept away softly lest the sick man should be disturbed.

Day by day the strong, stout frame dwindled and shrunk away, consumed by burning fever; the hard hands grew pale and soft; the dark, coarse face lengthened and whitened; until, one bright morning, as his mother sat beside him, thinking how strangely unlike he was to his old self, the closed eyes, grown wonderfully large and deep, were suddenly lifted and fixed on her face.

Startled by his sudden rousing from a sleep which the doctor had said would prove the turning point for life or death, she bent her face down to his, but did not speak. He lay for a moment looking at her; then a faint smile touched his white lips, and he whispered, "Dear Mother!" as he had used to whisper it when, a little, weary child, he had crept into her arms to rest.

He was quiet for a long while after that, glancing up now and then with an uncertain, wondering look around the unfamiliar room. But after a while his face grew troubled and distressed, and he began to move his head restlessly on the pillow.

"What is it, Ned dear, do you want something?" asked his mother, bending anxiously over him.

"The boy?" he whispered faintly. "The young feller from the Hall?"

"You mean you want him, dear?"

"Did they — did they hurt him — very bad?" he faltered feebly.

"No, they never hurt him a bit. He's been here every day since you've been sick, as watchful and kind as if you'd been his brother. But you mustn't talk, Ned dear, for you've been very sick. Take a little sleep now."

He closed his eyes obediently, and the happy old mother sat beside him, refusing all Mrs. Marsh's entreaties that she would take some rest, with the reply that it rested her to look at him sleeping so softly. And she was right; nothing could have been a sweeter rest to that heart, worn and weary with terrible fear and dread, than to watch the calm face upon the pillow, — the face which for three long weeks she had seen wild, and tortured with pain.

Then followed days and days of such infantile weakness as the man, never having within his recollection been ill before, could not comprehend. Days when he could not turn his head, nor lift his hand without aid; days when a child's voice in the street, or the creeping of a fly over the white counterpane, annoyed and distressed him.

But little by little strength came again; and one afternoon, as Dr. Buford sat beside his bed, with his fingers on his wrist, he said, —

"You are coming on finely, Bailey. I don't know but that I'll let you see a visitor to-day. Would you like it?"

"Is it Mr. Austin?" asked Bailey, eagerly. "I've been a wantin' to see him the worst kind."

"Well, he is waiting in the garden now. I will bring him in."

"Don't stay more than five minutes," said

the doctor, as having called Austin into the house he opened the door of Edward's room to let him pass in, " and be very cautious."

" Well, Bailey," said Frank cheerfully, coming to the bedside and taking one of Edward's hands in both his own, " you don't look quite as strong as you once did."

" No, not quite, but I'm a gainin'. I 'spose I never looked just like this afore;" and he glanced with a sort of compassionate smile at the thin, pale hand which lay in Frank's.

" A pretty white hand for a man, isn't it?" said Austin, giving it a little pat, " and not quite able to-day to hold a great fellow like me back from a crowd of enemies. But never mind, it will strengthen every day; strengthen too, I hope, for service in a better cause than mine. Let it grow strong, Bailey, but keep it white."

The man looked up, his sunken eyes scanning the boy's face wonderingly at first; then with a quick, intelligent look flashing from them, he said, —

"Ay, I know what you mean; know the need of it too better than you do, perhaps. It ain't easy work, boy."

"I know it is not," replied Frank, gravely. "But we have a Master to whom all things are easy," he added, with a smile, "and He will help us. What lovely flowers these are! Who sent them to you?"

"The little lady up to the Manor-House," said Bailey; as Frank, afraid of exciting him too much, bent over a beautiful basket of flowers which stood on a table beside the bed. "Folks is so good to me I don't scarcely know myself."

"They want to help me to thank you," said Austin. "I must go away now, or the doctor will not let me come again; but I cannot go without trying to tell you that from my heart I pray God to bless you for risking your life for me. You have suffered greatly on my account, Bailey; and if the time ever comes when I can repay the debt, you will find that my gratitude is full and true. Good-by."

"Good-by. Will you be down around these parts any time soon?"

"Oh, yes; I shall want to know every day how you are."

"Well, come in, if you don't mind, and sit a bit."

He lay looking after the boy as he went out, and turned his head on the pillow to watch him pass up the village street; then he lifted the wasted hand which had been so kindly noticed, held it up to the light, and turned it about as if studying it.

"Keep it white," he said thoughtfully. "Little he knows how black it has been. Little he knows either what it'll be to keep it white. And yet — I do believe — wouldn't the old woman be glad though?"

"The old woman" coming in at that moment, rather anxious lest his first interview with Frank might have proved too much for his strength, had her fears calmed at the first glance.

"Why, how nice you look!" she exclaimed, stroking the hair back from his forehead. "The young gentleman's done you good, I'm thinkin'. He's as fine a young man as ever I see, Ned."

"Yes, he's pretty fair. I'm tired, mother;" and seeing that he did not want to talk, she smoothed his pillows, and taking up her sewing sat down in the window.

Meantime Frank's adventure had caused no small stir in the village. The constables had come to him for intelligence with regard to the assaults upon himself and Bailey; but the only clue he could give them was the information that the voice of the man whose hand had covered his eyes was like that of William Simpson, and his belief that it was he who had attacked Bailey; but as some one else had taken Simpson's place, blindfolding him just as the latter had done, he could give no certain intelligence.

When Bailey was well enough to be questioned, he could furnish them with no more reliable testimony. He remembered the main facts of the occurrences of the evening, but could give no definite account of the participants in them, confusing the scene at the mill-pond with that at the tavern, in a manner which rendered investigation utterly hopeless.

But one point was gained that Frank had not hoped for. The officers, annoyed and somewhat chagrined to find that the originators of such a disturbance should escape without detection, gave Austin their word that he should be troubled with no farther interference in his plans. And more than that, their word was faithfully kept.

Dr. Drayton, on hearing that a constable would be stationed in the entry, just outside the door of Frank's room, every Sabbath afternoon, gave his consent to the continuance of the meetings; and the very circumstance of the strong opposition he had encountered, the news of which had of course spread all through the village, brought such a company into that little room as it had never held before. For the first few Sabbaths it was crowded to overflowing, benches having to be placed in the hall outside; and even after the excitement died away, the attendance was larger than it had ever been before.

One afternoon as Frank sat among the audience, it being Laurence Bronson's turn to conduct the services, he heard a little movement at the door; and looking up, saw Edward Bailey coming in with his mother, who looked as if her cup of happiness were filled to overflowing. After the meeting was dismissed, seeing that Bailey seemed waiting for him, Frank crossed the room to speak to him. As he grasped his hand, congratulating him on being with them once more, Edward said, with an awkward twisting of his shoulders, but with the light of an honest purpose in his eyes, —

"I thought as how I'd like to come once agen. I'm a goin' up to the lake with the old woman to-morrow to help along there. She wants me pretty bad, and — and — well, I guess my hands'll be more like to keep whiter if I'm out o' this here."

Little by little, as month after month passed on, the meetings in Mrs. Tracy's room began to tell on the tavern at the Corner. A constable, close at hand every Sabbath afternoon, made a very considerable difference in the proceedings outside the walls of the house; and within, one after another began to be missed. Simpson had disappeared, not having been seen since the night of the attack upon Austin. Bailey was gone; and Bailey's defection had carried off two or three more of the habitual loungers.

For three or four years the tavern still stood

there, and Milward still sold his poison to all who would buy, of whom there were only too many left; but after that autumn and winter the Corner was a different place; and five years later, coming back to Graydon on a visit, Frank Austin sat down one Sabbath morning in a church built on the site of the little house in which he had first lifted his voice in his Master's service, and heard one of his old school-mates preach a sermon from that Master's own promise: —

"Blessed are they which do hunger and thirst after righteousness: for they shall be filled."

www.ingramcontent.com/pod-product-compliance
Lightning Source LLC
Chambersburg PA
CBHW020843160426
43192CB00007B/762